When
Death
Takes a Father

When Death Takes a Father

by

Gladys Kooiman

BAKER BOOK HOUSE
Grand Rapids, Michigan

To

all who must walk
the lonely road of widowhood . . .

With special thanks to my four
lovely daughters, whose loving hands
made this book possible . . .

To my four lively sons who provided
me much raw material . . .

To the Baker Book House, for their
ready assistance and encouragement . . .

And to my dear friend, Wilma,
who started it all.

Preface

The death of a loved one, under any circumstances, is a shattering and sobering experience, but when the father of a family of ten is removed by the cold hand of death, a situation filled with pathos is created.

Mrs. Gladys Kooiman encountered just such a situation and was first invited to share her experience with readers of *Christian Home and School.* Recognizing the human interest and helpfulness inherent in her magazine articles, the publishers of this book urged her to write a complete story in book form. The result is a personal narrative that is not only interesting but also enlightening and instructive.

Those who find themselves in similar situations find this book helpful in meeting day-to-day crises brought on by the absence of a husband and father. Pastors, counselors, and social workers will find this book useful in understanding the plight of the widow with children, and rendering the kind of assistance which is needed. Relatives and friends of those who have experienced the trauma which accompanies the death of a father will discover its helpfulness in understanding the widow's world.

This is an outstanding book not only because of its poignant narrative and its helpfulness to others, but also because it points the reader to the fact that true comfort in times of bereavement is found through the avenues of faith and trust in God.

THE PUBLISHERS

Contents

PART ONE

We Loved, We Laughed, We Wept 11

  1 "The Pantry" 13

  2 "Critically Serious" 17

  3 "Mama, Mama!" 25

  4 Uneaten Birthday Cakes 30

  5 Living the Present 35

  6 To Be or Not To Be — Realistic 46

PART TWO

Without Father 55

  7 "We Lost Daddy Too!" 57

  8 On Making Boys into Men 64

  9 Speaking of Daddy 69

 10 Living Joyfully 72

PART THREE

Walking the Widow Road 81

 11 If I Can Just Once 85

 12 Loved and Lost 89

13   Nearsighted Vision   94

14   I Was a Stranger   104

15   Who Takes Advantage of the Widow   113

16   Who Cares?   119

17   Lonely and Alone   129

18   Not for Fixing Faucets   133

19   My Cows Are Not For Sale   138

20   Either Rich or Poor   144

21   The Third Choice   149

PART FOUR

Life Calls Again   155

22   Things Are Looking Up   157

*I*T'S FUNNY ABOUT SHOES! Shoes had always held a fascination for me: a symbol perhaps of life and activity. How frequently, after long weary days, I had been revitalized by the sight of the toddler's shoes. Then, smiling within and refreshed by the memory of the busy little feet that filled them, I wondered about the future destiny of these little feet — Where would they go, and would they walk for God?

It had not been particularly difficult to distribute my husband's dress shirts, trousers, and overcoat immediately after the funeral to his relatives who would be leaving soon for their homes some hundreds and more miles distant. But there was one article — his slippers — the ones he had been wearing moments before his death, which burned a hole in my consciousness and which I could neither give away nor forget. These slippers I did not possess. I had made two attempts to regain them from the funeral home, but it was not until several weeks after my beloved's death that I finally retrieved them, carelessly stuck into an old crumpled paper bag.

How eagerly I had clutched them, drawing them out with a tenderness it would be difficult to explain. With slow, measured steps I walked to his chair and placed them beside it. And they were empty — they were empty —

I think it was then that the realization first really took hold of me that I was alone with the responsibility of eight young children — and that I must carry on. God, knowing my weakness and my "frame," did not bring the full challenge to me all at once, but served it piecemeal, and every day with it His grace.

Part One

We Loved,
We Laughed,
We Wept

CHAPTER ONE

"The Pantry"

WHO CAN COUNT all the external incidents and internal forces at work to cause two people walking separately to meet and love? I suppose, in a way we could hold Pieter de Hooch, a mid-seventeenth century painter, responsible for our ever having walked together at all. Yet, if it had not been for Nazism and World War II, we might never have met at "The Pantry" and been influenced by it to choose each other as life partners.

We were students at Calvin College, Grand Rapids, Michigan, when it all began. For months I had entered classroom No. 17 as he (Marvin) left it. Every Tuesday and Thursday morning we brushed past one another; never once did we "see" each other — until one November day.

That day was a beautiful autumn Saturday. The occasion was a display of original masterpieces by famous Dutch artists at Detroit. These famous works had been stolen and then recovered from German salt mines by American occupational forces after World War II.

I was taking a course in Dutch art, something I was not particularly interested in, but it did nicely round out a minor in my education course. Until that time I had been subjected primarily to Italian art, especially that of the Renaissance. It had always left me cold. My practical realism could not pretend to appreciate its flowery, fanciful romanticism. It was with real joy and exhilaration that I discovered the refreshing, realistic works of Dutch painters.

Through the inspiration of my professor, a little man full of big ideas, I met art for the first time. From that point on I could not only appreciate great masterpieces, but also truly enjoy them. I particularly liked Rembrandt — his people were real people. I loved Vermeer — his talent at defining the quality of things and the spaces around them drew me time and time again. The serenity and air of freshness and purity, usually created by light streaming from a window, seemed to flow over everything. It touched my soul with a sense of peace.

Imagine the thrill I felt when our class was advised that arrangements were being made to allow all those of us interested to attend this exhibit, and then the dismay when I further learned that "all" that was required of us was a mere five-dollar train fare. While I did not lack interest, I did lack the necessary five dollars!

During the school year I managed to earn my room and board, but spending money had to come from the pittance left after tuition and money for clothes had been extracted from my summer wages. So earnestly did Professor Van Andel desire our attendance, that when he learned of our plight (I wasn't the only student lacking five dollars), he actually bribed several young men from

14

his Dutch language course into driving their cars to Detroit for two dollars per passenger. Even then the trip seemed costly, especially after mentally computing the fare plus the cost of meals along the way. The problems of money — or rather the lack of it — was a real one. "Someday, when I finished college — or when I married . . ." — in my youthful naïveté, wealth lay just around the corner.

Words fail me in describing the utter delight and rapture which engulfed me at this first encounter with those masterpieces — originals I had never dreamed I'd see. How far short the black and white prints, and even the colored ones we were using in class, fell in duplicating the irresistible lustre and beauty of those works! I had only one quarrel with those viewing them: everyone was in too much of a hurry to take in adequately their exquisite beauty. Forty works of supreme accomplishment deserved more than an hour or two of scant contemplation.

Upon nearing the end of the line, my glance was caught by "The Pantry." Erroneously I seized upon it as a Vermeer. Actually de Hooch was a "superficial" Vermeer; he used many of the same techniques. I suppose it was de Hooch's use of sunlight streaming from a kitchen window which caused me to identify it incorrectly. However, disappointment at my error in the identification of the master did not dampen nor lessen my enthusiasm for the scene before me. A sensation of warmth and coziness filled me as my attention was drawn by the love displayed in the mother's face as she handed her small daughter the blue pitcher of milk. The painting spoke of gentleness, softness. The blue and white tiled floor shone with cleanliness and spotlessness. The feeling of purity and wholesomeness created by the soft clear light captured me.

15

Utter delight at discovered beauty is never complete for me unless it is shared. I have always felt an urgent need to include a loved one in my joys and delights. It is not surprising that in my exuberance I found myself asking my friend, "Doesn't it look inviting, like home should be?" as I pointed out all the high spots of interest. "It almost makes me a little homesick," I spilled out with a tearful sigh.

Someone had been listening to our emotional conversation. Years later Marvin (he had been one of the drivers) still teased me about my love for Dutch art. "You didn't sell me on it, Hon," he was to say. "Oh, it's all right, I guess, if you like that stuff, but you certainly sold me on something, *you.* You were the wife I had to have," he explained. "You were there, a part of that picture."

Due most likely to the very fact that Marvin *knew* I was going to be his, and that independent I knew no such thing, our courtship was one of many ups and downs. Marvin's faith and persistence never wavered. Eighteen months later we were at the altar repeating to one another "Till death do us part."

Why did that parting come so soon? Didn't "till death" imply a whole lifetime, until one is ready to die? Fifteen years — only fifteen years! But then, would fifty, sixty, or even more years have been long enough? Does the time ever come when love is completely satisfied to part?

16

CHAPTER TWO

"Critically Serious"

OURS WAS NOT THE PERFECT MARRIAGE, the perfect love. In fact, we were very much an ordinary family with common ups and downs and differences.

There was Marvin: immaculately tidy, careful, neat in the smallest details. Then there was I, the one to leave the cap off the toothpaste tube, or a bottom dresser drawer open just far enough for him to catch his toe under. Dad was the one to take things slowly and surely. I, in contrast, could do things much more quickly, but I frequently had to find the time to do them over again — much to the irritation of both of us. Marvin was the introvert, I the extrovert; he the pessimist, I the all-too-naïve optimist; he the indecisive, doubtful Thomas, I the impetuous, impulsive Peter. It would be difficult to venture a guess as to whether he suffered more from insecure contemplation and decision-making than I with my regrets about too-hasty action. There were times we both had seizures of impatience with each other and with life in general. Marvin was easily discouraged when we seemed to be sliding backwards financially — that was most of the time. Sometimes I felt like a stack of neatly folded diapers, well worn with the monotonous routine of daily chores.

Many common qualities did knit our lives and love, though, in spite of our personality differences. We found a common delight in the quiet, the serene. Marvin had seen our home in the atmosphere that Pieter de Hooch depicted on canvas with light and shadow, blues and yellows. Our basic natures had truly met there.

We shared a common culture, too. Both of us came from Dutch backgrounds, and both from farms — Marvin in southwestern Minnesota and I from a mid-Wisconsin dairy farm. Perhaps the roots of our common love for nature can be traced to our early years in a rural setting. On many, many of our dates before marriage (and frequently afterwards) we could be found seeking out lovely paths in nearby woods, or unusual scenery away from the well-traveled highways. Marvin could sit and study a beautiful maple or a stately elm by the hour. Classical music played a close second among our loves. Not surprisingly, my first Christmas gift from him was a long-playing record of Debussy's *The Afternoon of a Fawn*. His gift from me? Sections of Handel's *Messiah*. Usually we attended local concerts alone — just the two of us. I was always secretly glad we had enough music appreciation to recognize and enjoy good music but not enough skill to judge every little flaw in the sharps and flats, thereby robbing us of its beauty. Our quick clasp of each other's hand was the only expression of musical enjoyment we cared for or needed.

Our common love for children was one of the bonds

which bound us closest to one another. "We would have six," we decided long before we ever married. Actually God blessed us with eight, first four lovely daughters "all in a row": Linda, Emily, Marilyn, and Judy; and after a space of a few years followed four lively, busy boys, "all in a row," too: Howard, Merlin, David, and Jerry.

We shared a common faith. Both of us had been raised in God-fearing homes, within the wings of the Christian Reformed Church. In the early months of our marriage, Grandma Kooiman sent us a wall plaque inscribed with these words: "Home Sweet Home — Where Each Lives for the Other and Both Live for God." It has hung there on my kitchen wall ever since, sometimes more of a grim reminder of what our home should have been rather than representing what it actually was. But invariably when we began to measure up to it we found our loads lifted, our differences soothed, and our home the kind of place we wanted it to be.

No, our home was not the perfect home. We had our good days and our crabby ones. The dad-shouted-at-mom, mom-scolded-daughter, daughter-slapped-brother, and brother-kicked-the-cat days. When the air wasn't too brittle someone would label us the Krabby Kooimans — other days we just thought so and left it at that.

Our home had more than the usual number of irritating empties: the empty catsup bottle, the jam jar (in fact Dad called them his Katzenjammer kids). There was always the empty sugar bowl by the time it reached Dad's cooling coffee cup, and the empty bandaid box. (Wounds always looked so much more dignified when covered with a patch or two. They had a miraculous way of diminishing pain too.) And the empty bank account!

And the brokens! The broken living room window,

with a hole a little larger than a baseball, broken fingers and toes, broken-off wheels from little toy trucks, and broken *hearts* over uncurly permanents that turned out into tight ringlets.

We never missed the ordinary bouts of flu, colds, and measles. Once, as I was caring for six very ill, mumpy children all at once, I wondered if we really needed such an extra amount of the ordinary things.

We had several of the "only-can-happen-at-our-house" incidents, too. In whose house but ours would four young boys think of salvaging the Elmer's glue from its broken container, pouring it into Mom's empty shampoo jar and then leaving it out where some tidy person would inadvertently place it back on the bathroom shelf? In whose house but ours would a stray cat that looked "so hot" be cooled off in a food freezer, or where but in my kitchen would a young helper carefully pour all the salt into the sugar container just before I decided to bake two lovely rhubarb meringue pies we would never eat?

Not a perfect love, marriage, and home — but it was good. It was the place where we lived and loved, laughed, and learned.

Then the blow came — unexpectedly. Marvin, who had never been ill in all his life, was suddenly hospitalized with a frightening illness — Not seriously ill," the heart specialist had said, "but *critically* serious, lady."

Specialists in every field came and went and shook their heads. X-rays, tests, more X-rays, and more tests followed while his life hung on a fine thread. After days of deliberation, the verdict was immediate surgery — open heart surgery to repair or replace a damaged heart valve and artery. Chances of survival: less than 50 per cent; length

20

of survival without surgery: hours, days, maybe weeks — No more. Several anxious days followed as surgeons attempted to locate an artificial valve large enough, and finally, after fruitless searching, found it would be necessary to have one manufactured. In fear and agony we awaited the possibly fatal day of surgery — yet our only hope. We did hope in spite of the fifty-fifty chance of survival. Up until that time only six surgical operations of this type had been attempted — not all of them successfully.

The surgery seemed endless. Hour after hour droned on, and a voice re-echoed over and over: "not serious — *critically* serious, lady." Seven hours dragged their feet before word came from the operating room where six leading specialists were bent upon saving one life — my husband's. I sat helpless, reading a book I remembered nothing of. I preferred the soothing, quiet effect to nervous, strained conversation with relatives who were sitting beside me. Hospital personnel had spent much time instructing both of us concerning post-operative matters, particularly stressing the fact that I must maintain a great deal of self-control if I were to be of any value in helping Marvin along the road to recovery. It was already much in demand. After seven agonizing hours, I heard only that Marvin was once again living by the power of his own heart beat. I was to learn later that the transition from the heart-lung machine back to his own heart proved to be nearly fatal. All the intricate exactness with which these doctors had cut away part of the aorta and repaired the faulty valve was nearly lost when his heart balked and refused to pick up its work again. Exactly ten and one-half hours after Marvin was rolled into the elevator, on his way to surgery, he was rolled back again. This time with tubes and instruments dangling from

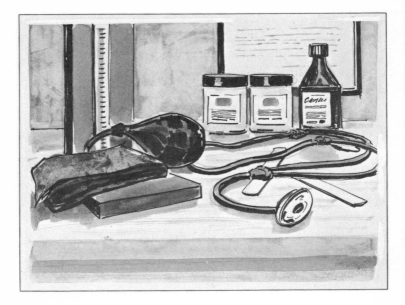

each bed post, devices for blood transfusions and intravenous feedings, apparatus I had never encountered before.

"The next ten days are crucial ones," the hospital informed me. "We must know where to reach you every minute of the day and night if you are not here on the floor." For seven days I stayed at his bedside.

Although Marvin was too ill to carry on a conversation, he became anxious and restless the moment he thought I wasn't there. Each day brought a measure of recovery for Marvin — each day brought me a deeper sensation of homesickness for the children. The seventh day Marvin seemed so much improved that I planned a quick trip to the hospital room the next morning to reassure myself that all was fine and then a quick trip home to see my babies.

I was totally unprepared that Friday morning for the

regression that had taken place overnight. Walking into his room, no one needed to tell me that my plans would not develop. Three doctors and three nurses, fighting with all the ingenuity of modern science to save a life, were standing at his bedside. They did all they could, then left one by one for more surgery and other patients. The last surgeon to leave said quietly, "We've done all we can — the rest is up to God."

I can't remember praying — the groanings were too deep for words. I felt better when the special nurse advised me that I could help. "Talk — talk to him even when you don't think he's hearing you," she demanded. "You must talk him into living." What does one talk about to the dying and not bring up the subject? I began relating little incidents about the children, things I had been told that they had said and done the past few days. When I mentioned Jerry or David, I saw a little flicker, ever so slight; I knew he was hanging on, fighting. This was my cue. On and on I went, repeating the children's names and the little incidents over again when I couldn't remember new ones. Twice, just as life seemed to ebb away, it was just the names of the children which seemed to call him back. So vividly did these sink into his consciousness, that once he smiled and asked me in delirium, "What did the kids say when I rode by?" This is the one and only time that I completely lost all semblance of self-control. The quick-thinking nurse answered for me, "What do *you* think?" I wept, and my arms ached for my baby.

The symptoms were so minute, so subtle, and yet I could clearly discern that death was playing a losing role. It was battling a very ill man armored with eight kids who wouldn't let him go. I never convinced Marvin later, after recovery, that the children had not been up to his hospital room that day. He knew they were there. He saw them as he moved by.

A glorious homecoming took place many weeks later. Marvin was greeted by eight pairs of eager, love-filled eyes pouring out love and devotion. It mattered not at all that he could not frolic or work. Dad was home. His chair was no longer empty; his slippers were filled again.

After a thorough post-operative examination six months later, renewed hope filled our hearts. The specialist was pleased at the measure of recovery. "Six months ago your outlook would have been less than six weeks of life left," the doctor exclaimed. "If nothing further develops, you may even look forward to some measure of normal activity and light work by spring." We were so elated at the news that I almost missed the ominous "if."

"The if's doctor?"

The doctor cautiously felt his way. Finally he said, "When we operate for appendicitis, we take the appendix away. Never again is there a re-occurrence of that difficulty. We repaired only a very small section of the aorta system, you know. Sometimes other weak spots occur. These we cannot foresee."

"What do you suggest we do, doctor?"

After a long pause he said quietly, "Nothing more — just live today — live the present."

CHAPTER THREE

"Mama, Mama"

VEN AS I SLOWLY AND PAINFULLY REACHED OUT to still the shrill alarm which had awakened me one morning, I recalled that the day should be something special.

It was Christmas and the day appeared as gloomy and dreary as I felt. Outdoors the wind was howling; snow was falling and heavy drifts were mounting in our drive and road. "Weren't things bad enough without the weather cooperating to make matters worse?" my heart cried. There was small chance of even getting to church or to Grandmother's for dinner!

I turned at the sound of, "Merry Christmas, Mom," and eager little feet behind me.

"Merry? Merry Christmas?" How could it be merry for me, when all our elevated hopes for ever being a normal family again had been crumpled and splintered like the ornament I had dropped while decorating the tree.

Things were looking up until the day before — December 24 — Marvin's birthday, too! In anticipation I had baked his angel food cake, and already before breakfast it was perched upside down on a catsup bottle to cool.

The family gathered in the kitchen, later than usual because of school vacation. Little David still needed his shoes tied and asked his daddy for help. The rest of us were seated around the table, waiting impatiently before our cooling breakfasts. All eyes were suddenly riveted upon Dad as we saw him groping for David's shoes and ties and then toying with them in a perplexed manner, as if he had never seen plain, ordinary shoestrings before and hadn't the slightest idea what to do with them. Next we saw him slump to the floor before us.

In contrast to later strokes, which were to occur over and over again, this was just a slight one. Within a few minutes only slurred speech remained, and by the time the doctor arrived, virtually all outward symptoms had vanished. Yet, because we had been forewarned of just such a possibility, this first incident brought with it a message clearly written: all our efforts to prolong Marvin's life would be only temporary measures at best.

Although Marvin was not hospitalized, we were ordered to keep him absolutely quiet. His cake, still undecorated, was carried carefully to the basement freezer for another day. Cakes were to become linked with tragedy for quite some time.

In an effort to purchase as much as possible with the few meager dollars we set aside for Christmas spending, we decided to put off all shopping until the last few hours before closing time on Christmas Eve, when merchants, anxious to dispose of their inventories, began slashing prices. We had planned to go together, but now I faced the task alone. My heart was so heavy that my feet could barely drag it along.

Pleading electric signs and neon lights glared upon the icy street. Snow was falling, not the soft, fluffy cotton-like flakes I always loved, but hard, sharp beads that pelted downward, burning and stinging, hurled about by a malicious wind which penetrated even the heavy black seal coat I was wearing.

Everyone rushing in and out of the stores seemed bent upon beating the five o'clock closing hour to purchase the little but urgent items still needed — some more wrapping paper perhaps, a gift for some one whose name was omitted from the list, or extra bulbs and baubles for that empty spot on the tree. A mother rushed past, dragging a trailing, tired child by the hand, scolding, "Well, I told you to stay home with your daddy." Gay teen-agers whizzed around the corner, screeching on the two right wheels of a little red convertible, celebrating the beginning of school vacation. An elderly gentleman swaggered and wavered uncertainly along the store fronts. He shouted, "Merry Christmas, Merry Christmas," and waved his black tattered cap at passers-by, obviously having begun his kind of celebration a bit ahead of schedule. On the street corner, Santa Claus, with a voice husky with fatigue, still called out Christmas greetings. Drawn clerks at the store counters eagerly watched the clock make its way ever so slowly through the last few hours, while bidding a "Merry Christmas" to their customers, with faces smiling as if frozen that way. In contrast, a heavy black sound box attached to a street lamp blared out above all the din, "Silent night, All is calm," and "Peace, good will to men." I was oblivious to the spirit of it, very much a lost and wandering child in unfamiliar surroundings, intent only upon the few small gifts I still had to choose and purchase alone.

Christmas Eve brought no emotional release either. That evening our children always performed for their mothers and fathers in the annual church program. If there ever was one parent who had "all eyes" for his own children on stage and had a difficult time refraining from shouting, "Look, that's my son," or "That's my daughter," it was Marvin. He was proud of his offspring to a fault, in fact, to the point of downright conceit. How he loved children's programs! But that Christmas Eve he did not see them. I attended the program, but tears so blurred my vision while sitting there alone in the pew, I didn't see them either!

I distinctly remember the Christmas morning that followed. In spite of everything, I tried to create a cheerful atmosphere for the children's sake. I dreaded to awaken them, knowing my "Merry Christmas — time-to-get-up" greeting would be only forced gaiety. I decided to delay informing them that Christmas church services and dinner at Grandma's weren't likely unless it stopped blowing and snowing very soon. There was really no point in spoiling their day until after our breakfast and gift-opening ceremonies.

I did manage a special breakfast — hot cinnamon rolls, scrambled eggs, a pretty Christmas bread with icing and red and green cherries on top, hot chocolate, and large expensive oranges — the kind we seldom tasted at our house.

The children chattered expectantly regardless of the shadow of cold hovering over us. They awaited the gifts they couldn't guess, rehashed all the awkward incidents in the program the evening before, and planned the fun they would have later with their cousins.

Neither Marvin nor I had spoken of our keen disappointment, yet even as our gaze met across the table, each knew that this might well be our last Christmas together. I choked back the tears, and a lump of Christmas bread stuck in my throat.

It seems that when one is cast into the deep darkness of despair even miniscule rays of joy seem bright and beautiful. One of them reached in just then. My tiny nine-month-old son, wanting my attention and failing to receive it, said "Mama," and then in sudden awareness of his first successful word, and spurred on by the entire cheering family, repeated over and over again, "Mama, Mama."

Not one of my eight had ever spoken that lovely word so young; each waited until many months after having learned *Daddy*. The choked tears now freely tumbled over the sticky, buttered fingers that caressed my face, and he repeated in utter delight, "Mama, Mama!"

As if on cue, the sun peeked from behind the clouds just then. In the distance roaring engines of busy snow plows reassured us.

My thoughts were suddenly directed back to another mother and the birth of a son who was to bring real, lasting joy to the hearts of the entire world, not just to one complaining mother.

And then it was Christmas — a *Merry* Christmas — in my soul.

CHAPTER FOUR

Uneaten Birthday Cakes

I VIVIDLY REMEMBER THE NEXT SEVERAL MONTHS in terms of birthday cakes. Each day after Christmas, Marvin seemed a little stronger, so that by the end of the week we decided it would be safe to celebrate his belated birthday on New Year's Day. New Year's Eve the children brought up the cake. They drooled as I decorated it with pretty blue icing, pink candles, and little silver sugar balls left from Christmas. Eager eyes watched every move, while sticky fingers licked the frosting spoon, beaters, and bowl as I trussed a big fat turkey (a gift from Marvin's former employer), made dressing, and pared potatoes for tomorrow's dinner.

Just moments after I slipped the turkey into the oven early New Year's morning, Marvin went into a second spell, this time a more serious one. Two hours later he was under intensive care once again at the University Hospital. Although the children at home ate the cake that noon for dessert, they never lit the candles! "We didn't feel like it," they explained later.

March 19th was the baby's first birthday. A dear friend brought a bunny cake, white and fuzzy with coconut, large pink maraschino cherries for eyes, and tall pink ears. A large pink candle rested on the middle of the bunny's back. But once again we brushed past a lovely cake sitting on the side board in the kitchen. We were on our way to the hospital!

The sixth of July, Merlin's birthday, dawned bright and clear. It was still a part of the 4th of July weekend vacation, and Marvin's brother suggested going fishing.

Marvin and the younger boys enthusiastically prepared the fishing gear while the older children quickly performed early morning chores. Dad was so excited over the outing he could hardly allow time for preparation. In very short order the gang was off. Only Baby and Mom remained home to "bake the cake."

"Surely nothing could go wrong on such a lovely morning," I decided as I got out the mixer and eggs. It was not to be so, for even before I placed the cake on the oven rack, the telephone informed me that once more a birthday cake would go uneaten, for Marvin had collapsed at the fishing stream and was even now on his way to the hospital. Several forlorn little faces met me at the door a few minutes later. Dejectedly they set down their bucket of fish — "Fishing was so good, too," one stated sadly. "We caught twenty-one in that little while." My heart ached at their obvious disappointment.

This time I sat at his bedside hour after hour as anxious nurses hovered over him and grave doctors shook their heads. "We've tried everything, and there is no response," Dr. Leonard finally admitted. "If he lives through this stroke he'll never make another."

31

Sisters on duty tried to prepare me for the inevitable by asking if all necessary matters were in order at home. I stood helplessly by, not even sure Marvin knew that I was there with him. Each moment seemed to pull him nearer death. Again life hung on a fragile thread for days, and then after every shred of hope vanished, the tiniest response was noted. Although many areas of his body were affected, as well as parts of the brain, it soon became apparent that Marvin was improving. He would be coming home once more. We hoped it would be before Linda's birthday, but the doctors shook their heads and suggested that it was still too early to make any predictions.

Several days later kind hospital personnel did make arrangements for the entire family to visit him in a private waiting room on the first floor. Since every time we baked a birthday cake, Marvin invariably was suddenly snatched away to a hospital, this time we decided to reverse the order and bring the cake to Dad. Originally we had planned to eat it together, but as I mentally envisioned four little sons balancing trays of sticky cake on Sunday-pants knees, I talked them into eating their cake at home and just bringing Dad a large slice. Carefully we arranged a large wedge on a saucer covered with a lacy doily. A pretty pink rosette holding a single candle was placed on center, and then just to make sure it wouldn't be left behind, it was covered with a foil dome and placed on the front seat of the car.

At last we were off — eight children, brushed, scrubbed, dressed (two of them redressed for a second time), all excited at seeing their daddy again. The ride to the hospital was a short one, and we were almost there when Howard

called, "Hey, Ma, where's the cake? I don't see it back here."

"Don't worry," I snapped, "the cake's right here on the front se_____t!" It was on the front seat all right, well pressed under the bottom of one plump little girl. It was useless to ask "how could such a thing happen?" as useless as asking how any other impossible thing happens in a house with eight children. They simply do. Fortunately Dad was far more interested in his children than he was in cake, and he assured them that angel food cake pressed with pink whipped cream would still be a delicious dessert with his supper.

I simply could not bake another cake for my birthday in August. The girls didn't feel it was quite appropriate for Mom to bake her own anyway and prepared a lovely three-layer chocolate cake ("with steps," David whispered) as a special surprise. No unfavorable incidents occurred this time, and seemingly as the cake spell was broken, so too was Marvin's for the next several months. Yet, I still breathe a little prayer before I begin an angel food cake.

CHAPTER FIVE

Living the Present

MY HANDS MOVED MECHANICALLY, feeding the baby, peeling potatoes, washing dishes, while my feet carried me automatically from stove to table to counter. The initial days of shock following re-occurrence of Marvin's difficulties were followed by a poignant disbelief. Surely the doctor had to be wrong. "These little spells couldn't be that serious," I argued. "These couldn't be the 'if's' the specialist had spoken of."

Gradually, however, as the seriousness of the situation made its impact upon me, I was forced to admit that they were the if's the doctor had in mind. With the heightened realization that Dad might not be with us very much longer, I re-evaluated former drives, values, and aims, and found them wanting. Bitterly I realized that Marvin and I had both been so busy, he with the business of providing for us, and I with all the innumerable household duties entailed with a large family, that we had become little more than wound-up time clocks. Providing for a large family, of course, is no small task, but somehow I began to question the merit of so much ambition and industriousness. Time and ambition had become tyrannical masters, "and what for?" I asked, as I saw much of our hard-earned funds drained away by mounting medical bills.

Idealistically, I recalled those first words spoken by Marvin's surgeon a few months earlier, "Live the present." We would live it now — savoring every morsel we had left. There were so many things we had always *meant* to do. Time and again, we told ourselves, "Next year we'll take that trip, but next year always found us even more tied down and busier than ever.

There were valid excuses, of course. Many of those years had brought a tiny baby, or else one was on the way — either would have made a trip uncomfortable. Dairy farming made trips difficult, too. Long rows of dairy cattle are quite insistent upon their morning and evening schedules. A farmer in our area hesitates to ask neighbors to take over, for they too have long lines of bawling bossies to attend to. Few of his city friends are either capable of taking over such chores, or they are not willing to keep the 5 A.M. and 5 P.M. schedules that milk cows insist upon, and also sandwich their regular city job between. Yet, now that Marvin was incapacitated, we found that help could be obtained, not just for a few hours, but for months at a time.

It was Judy's geography lesson that gave the impetus toward that first trip — Chicago. "Dad, what's the Chicago Board of Trade all about?" she asked one evening shortly after dinner.

"Now, that's one place I always meant to visit," Dad explained. I heard a little echo: "Live the present." Time and time again, in our first years together, we had promised

36

ourselves, "Someday we will stop and visit here," as we passed through the outskirts of Chicago on our way from our prior home in Michigan to my former one in Wisconsin. That "someday" never had emerged from our dreams.

"Next week is Teachers' Convention, Dad. Do you suppose we could manage a trip then, with the children?" I ventured cautiously.

With even the slightest hint of encouragement from Marvin, I began making preparations for the trip. I am always amazed how many hurdles can be met and dealt with when the will to do so is present. Since we were already engaging someone to perform the chores, obstacle number one was already overcome.

Planning began with a hasty letter to the Chicago Chamber of Commerce for information concerning points of interest, expenses involved with various exhibitions, and the location of moderately-priced hotels. Aunt Millie, who formerly lived in Chicago, volunteered to chauffeur us, solving another difficulty. Marvin was no longer permitted to drive, and I was thoroughly frightened at the prospect of driving in the Loop. Aunty Jay gladly accepted the care of the two youngest children for those two days.

A closely-scheduled itinerary was a "must," first of all, in order to cram into forty-eight hours all the things we wanted to see, and secondly, because Aunt Millie would be taking our station wagon with her to the outskirts of the city, so she could visit old friends and neighbors while we went sight-seeing. This made it necessary to find a centrally-located hotel so we could reach the places of interest by foot. The ample materials sent by the Chamber of Commerce helped us to choose the YMCA, as it seemed to serve our needs best. Reservations were quickly sent for.

After much study the schedule looked somewhat like this:

THURS.	7:30 A.M.	Leave Home
	11:30 A.M.	Arrive at the Museum of Science and Industry
	4:00 P.M.	Aunt Millie drives us to the Y
	7:30 P.M.	See the Chicago Loop at night
FRI.	8:00 A.M.	Breakfast
	9:00 A.M.	Museum of Natural Science
	10:00 A.M.	Shedd Aquarium
	11:00 A.M.	Planetarium — Special Demonstration — Do not be late!
	12:30 P.M.	Aunt Millie meets us for a picnic lunch at the park.
	2:00 P.M.	O'Hare Airport
	3:00 P.M.	Leave for Home

WILL I BE READY?

The financial hurdle demanded cooperation from everyone. I simply made the ultimatum — "Kids, we're going to Chicago to fill our heads — not our stomachs."

The one big expense we could not avoid, of course, was that for rooms. We did manage to scrimp a little by doubling four smaller children into two singles. We would have to cut corners everywhere else. With great care and patience I made the grocery list — enough to cover meals for two days — not many things too sweet, or too salty. These would mean endless thirst, excessive drinking of liquids, and no end of inconvenient "I-gotta-go" stops.

Urbanites will find it difficult to appreciate the wonder we "farmers" experienced as we viewed skyscrapers for the first time, or the thrill we experienced on our first escalator ride. We could only gasp bewilderingly at the noisy busyness and confusion of the big city.

The myriads of exhibits in the Museum of Science and Industry fascinated every member of the family. Joggling through the tunnel of the coal mine was exciting. The tour through the Nazi submarine absorbed the attention of everyone, and the model farm was examined carefully. The boys gleefully studied the mooing, glassy-eyed guernseys and holsteins, whose mechanically-operated movements approached reality. Seriously we climbed through the mammoth model of the human heart and studied the valve and aorta that had caused us so much concern. The excitement of the day had pushed the reality of Marvin's condition into the background, but the model heart at the museum brought a painful reminder that the day might come when Dad would no longer be with us to share in the excitement of discovery.

Our ears popped at the Y as we hurtled up nineteen floors in the elevator. So often did the boys find occasion for using it that the elevator operator became a warmly-greeted friend long before the evening was spent. How delightful and tempting those lovely, clean beds appeared to us — and we didn't have to make them. Squeals of laughter followed a cry of alarm at the children's first introduction to the shower. (Our bathroom at home boasts only a lion-pawed tub.) Howard, in excited anticipation, jumped into the shower in his stocking feet!

It was my carefully-packed lunches, with no allowances made for buying extra food (except for the Friday morning breakfast we had promised them at the cafeteria), which nearly proved our undoing. We had stopped for a picnic lunch at a wayside park just before reaching Chicago. As we left the car at the museum, each child was handed a neat lunch bag containing sandwiches, apples, potato chips, a candy bar, and a small plastic bag of sugar-coated cereals. This was to be our menu for the remainder of the day, until we reached the Y, where each would receive another similar bag. Imagine my chagrin when at the museum we were greeted everywhere with signs prohibiting the eating of food. After several complaints of hunger during the long walks in the museum, we decided to find the cafeteria. Because we hesitated to use the fine, clean facilities without buying anything, Dad suggested that we purchase a tall glass of lemonade for each. Purposely we chose a table quite remote from the counter and other customers, hoping to make our home-brought lunches as inconspicuous as possible. It was all for nothing.

"Count on *your* kids to show us up," Dad remarked dryly as we viewed the soggy mess we were leaving behind: Two upturned glasses of lemonade were busily soaking dried beef sandwiches and turning crisp cereal ovals into plump, fat donuts. I was too embarrassed at the moment to dispute the ill-chosen pronoun, *your*.

Imagine my complete bafflement later at the "Positively No Food Allowed" signs we found tacked up in our rooms at the Y. I was really disturbed when I discovered that the cafeteria had closed while we were resting. Food in the hand did little for empty stomachs.

This time the children quite unwittingly solved the dilemma. By the time I returned from a fruitless search for a place where we might eat, I was met by two excited rascals, their hungry tummies all but forgotten in the excitement of the new discovery — the fire escape. Their curious noses and busy fingers had discovered that with just a little push the door opened to "the best of the trip yet" — a panoramic view of the gigantic city in all its brilliant splendor. "Please, Mom, can't we just sit out there?" they begged. "It's so pretty — just look!"

Nineteen floors up did seem terribly high, and the steel-ribbed steps did seem a bit airy, but eventually I too was absorbed by the commanding scene before us. After several emphatic warnings about the dangerous height, and imposition of a few stern laws about pushing or shoving, I dashed back to our rooms to awaken Dad and invite him to join us. An insulated sandwich bag reminded me that we hadn't eaten as yet, and once again I studied the sign tacked to the wall. It said eating was not allowed in our rooms, but it did not mention fire escapes!

The children were actually awed into silence, drinking in the vastness of light, beauty, and color, while happily munching potato chips and crunching carrot strips and apples. As in the darkness I found Marvin's hand seeking mine, even as I reached for his, I was glad for the present day. The sharp cut into my finger as he pressed against my wedding rings was adequate testimony that he was "living the present" too.

All too quickly the spell was broken as the children clamored to get into the street for a walk. Although the nap had definitely revived Marvin's spirits, he was still obviously tired, so we measured our steps accordingly, strolling along leisurely. His left leg was causing him considerable difficulty, especially as he attempted to climb the high curbs. After one of these struggles he fumed good-naturedly, "No wonder they talk about Chicago drunks lying in the gutter — a sober man can hardly make it." The fact that I knew where we wanted to go, and that I held the map but couldn't recognize north from south, keeping us walking in the wrong direction most of the evening, did little to help matters. How silly we must have appeared to native Chicagoans, as corner after corner we paused beneath a street lamp to study our post-card map in order to ascertain why we weren't finding the places we were looking for.

The children's first cafeteria meal next morning proved almost as exciting as the German submarine trip at the museum. This time there were no spills, no messes. They did manage to draw considerable attention to themselves, however, as their big "farmer" appetites carried them for a second time along the cafeteria for an extra one-half serving of delicious French toast.

The remainder of our planned activities moved along smoothly. At noon Aunt Millie was greeted warmly by a tired, famished family, quite ready to get off their feet and repast on the picnic lunch she brought. The menu was a bit too familiar, but at least the sandwiches were fresh, the milk cold, and the coffee deliciously hot!

Evidently, what I meant to say before we left was, "We aren't going to Chicago to eat *expensively*," for we had consumed three boxes of sugar-coated cereals, two boxes of potato chips, sixteen candy bars, dozens of cookies, a large bag of celery sticks and carrot strips (our salads), over forty sandwiches, and one-half bushel of apples (our desserts). I can still see the smirk on Marvin's face as two pleading little sons begged, "Please, Mom, some mashed potatoes with lots of brown gravy for supper," only minutes after arriving home.

It was interesting to note that while each of us had thoroughly enjoyed the experience, few agreed upon which sights impressed us most. The older girls were especially impressed by the mine and submarine. Dad thought the special exhibit at the planetarium particularly beautiful. I remembered most vividly the enchanting scene from the fire escape. For the boys, the best part of all was the farm at the museum. They proved once again an old law of human nature, the tendency to relate with the familiar.

One very vivid impression that the younger children gained from the trip was not brought to my attention until several days later when Merlin observed, "Mommy, Negroes are Christians too, aren't they?"

"Why, of course," I quickly agreed, "but why did you happen to ask that?"

He proceeded to remind me of the Negro soloist who had sung at a short vesper service we had attended that first evening at the Y. I had all but forgotten it, in spite of the fact that she had made us "tremble" in her rendition of "Were you There?". She even sang "Jesus Loves Me," just for our children — the only ones present that evening. I blushed at Merlin's question. If there was one thing I hated, it was racial prejudice. I always stressed love and tolerance toward those of another race or creed. Yet my little ones had to stumble upon the one truth which makes all people equals, all men brothers — the Cross of Calvary — because I forgot to tell them.

A weekly newspaper from Marvin's home town, Edgerton, Minnesota, spawned plans for another trip the following summer. Cousins from there presented us with a year's subscription to it as an expression of thanks for hospitality they had received at our house during one of their trips. Marvin had been away from home for over fifteen years, and although Wisconsin had been his choice for beginning a dairy farm, I watched him eagerly scan the paper for familiar names and places — he still loved his home town, too. We had returned a few times, but usually only for short and often sad visits. Once it was for his mother's funeral, and again a few years later for that of a brother. Seldom had there been time to look up old friends or to revisit familiar scenes. Perhaps a visit back home would be good for him, and there was another wish I wanted to grant him — mountains.

While Wisconsin beauty never ceased to move Marvin, especially its brilliant, colorful autumn, he frequently expressed a longing desire to see mountains. Even as I mentally planned a visit to Minnnesota, I began toying with the idea of leaving the four little boys with relatives there, and going on to Denver, the home of one of Marvin's brothers. This would enable him to see those mountains as well as family. We even discussed a trip to California to visit still another brother, but skeptical friends and relatives felt that such a venture would prove far too strenuous for Marvin. We were deeply disappointed when the doctor disapproved of our Denver plans as well, because of the high altitude. After much discussion, and with hesitancy, he finally relented and agreed that perhaps we might go as far as the Black Hills in South Dakota. He stressed over and over the need to take the trip leisurely, with much rest, and with exacting instructions about the several medications Marvin was taking.

Upon our arrival in Edgerton, thoughtful aunts invited us into their homes for open-house sessions, and I believe everyone of Marvin's "cousins by the dozens," as well as every friend he had ever known, made a short call. We spent many hours with Marvin's friends, reliving nearly-forgotten adventures all over again. The entire family enjoyed revisiting special spots of interest with him too — the house where he was born, the school he attended, and especially the very corner where he was spanked by an angry Grandpa Kooiman because he had gone out riding with his new pony for many miles without informing his parents of his plans.

The Badlands along the way to the Black Hills fascinated us. Due to Marvin's insatiable curiosity, we found ourselves stopping at every lookout point to catch just another breathtaking view of this great, colorful spectacle of nature. We were equally thrilled by the four gigantic sculptured faces of our early American presidents at Mount Rushmore, probably more so because we had just recently finished reading the biography of Gutzon Borglum, the master artist with an uncanny ability to sculpt in colossal proportions.

But it was the Hills — black from a distance because of their dark green forestry — which elicited Marvin's unbounding enthusiasm. Over and over, as we approached this impressive scenery, he asked, "Could this be what mountains look like?" or, "Do you suppose mountains could be more beautiful?"

Marvin never got to see real mountains here below, but somehow I'm sure he has found them — The Everlasting Hills, singing praises to their Maker.

CHAPTER SIX

To Be or Not To Be — Realistic

*A*S THE CANDLE OF LIFE GREW SHORTER, and its flame began to flicker unsteadily as time progressed, I began to react as two distinct and often opposite personalities. For the sake of clarity I shall name them Idealistic Mary and Realistic Martha. Each brought her virtues and vices; together they carried me through a period of my life which is most precious in my memory, and yet the most painful and difficult.

Idealistic Mary moved about, leaving no stone unturned in making the most of "the present." When weather and health permitted, we took hikes, drives, and color tours — fishing and swimming too. Inclement weather found us spending hours reading great books together. Spiders wove their webs contentedly where ceilings and walls meet, and dust gathered undisturbed behind dressers and under beds. Tomorrow we would clean, today we would live!

Even as time and life took on new meaning, so did the spiritual verities. We found and took more time for family devotions, Bible study, and prayer. It seems strange, but at a time when death and loss loomed so near, we found truly thankful hearts for the first time in our lives. The very fact that life was still there at all made us especially conscious of the extra blessings. It was Idealistic Mary who made those last days so memorable and rich, almost tranquil. Somehow if she just cared enough, prayed earnestly, and lived deeply, everything would turn out all right.

Realistic Martha could not rest so easily. Even as Mary rejoiced in love and life, Martha would come tapping her on the shoulder with grim reminder, "Ah, yes, enjoy this while you *can.*" Sometimes she tugged at the heart strings as she scolded, "Two death warnings, my lady, you can't go on closing your eyes to the inevitable." Her long, pointed fingers jabbed harshly with, "What *if* Marvin had died after that first spell? Wouldn't you be in a fine fix now," and continued with, "Better prepare. Better prepare."

It was true. We certainly had neglected and been careless about several important matters. I was truly ill-prepared to carry on alone. Why, we didn't have a will! We had never seriously discussed what steps I should have to take if. . . . But then death hadn't really ever occurred as a threat to *us.*

Finding a good legal advisor wasn't difficult at all. Our attorney was a long-time, trusted family friend. It wasn't so difficult to get Marvin to his office either, once an appointment had been made. The attorney began by demanding to see a copy of all our legal papers, deeds to property, insurance policies, shares of stock in the local cooperative businesses, as well as our savings and checking account books at the bank. With meticulous care he examined each to make sure that all were in proper order. He particularly stressed that all accounts at the bank should read

Marvin and/or Gladys Kooiman. As a result, neither account was closed to me when Marvin died. To our complete surprise, he did not advise making a will at all. With estates as small as ours, he assured us, we would do much better with joint-tenancy ownership. Under this type of legal arrangement all real estate is listed as belonging to both partners. He also drew up a "bill of sale" listing all our personal property, which would make the survivor complete owner of such upon the death of the other. Although we were a bit skeptical of these foreign-sounding terms, we followed his suggestions completely, purely out of faith in his integrity. (Later, after Marvin's death, I found we had not been misled. The settling of the estate ran as smoothly and quickly and as satisfactorily as that afternoon trip to the lawyer.)

The full impact of the afternoon's business did not really hit me until the following evening. After Marvin became aware of the fact that I was unduly disturbed, I blurted out, "Look, Hon, you signed everything we own over to me in case of your death. Would you have done that if I hadn't been there with you this afternoon? Is this the way you really want it? Do you realize," I went on, "that this leaves the children penniless — that I could squander all your hard-earned money, leaving them unprotected?"

Marvin paused so long that I felt sure he had real misgivings about our afternoon's endeavor. Finally he broke the silence, pressed my hand in his, and uttered one of the most precious and shortest compliments he had ever paid me, "But Gladys, I *know* you."

Decisions! Is there ever a time in family or farm management that there isn't some pressing problem calling for solution? All through our married life we had chosen to make important decisions together. When it came to farm matters, I gladly catered toward Marvin's good judgment. Idealistic Mary liked it that way; so did Realistic Martha; but there came a day when Martha began to realize that this pattern might have to be broken in spite of Mary's disapproval.

As long as there had been encouraging signs and evidence that Marvin might recover from this illness, to the point where he might resume dairy chores again, we decided to hang on, to limp along the best we could. It had taken years of hard work, effort, and expense to build up our excellent dairy herd. Once disposed of, it would be too difficult and costly to replace. Limp along we did. Since Marvin was constantly in and out of the hospital, it was often necessary for me to take over the responsibility of farm management and the hired man. Good farm help was scarce. Dairy-farm income is simply inadequate to compete with wages paid by local industries. The long hours demanded by milk cows are hardly conducive toward drawing men who can obtain eight-hour shifts and five-day weeks. (Dairy cows never heard of Saturdays, Sundays, or holidays.) It never seemed to fail that our hired men would leave for better wages and hours when Marvin was in the hospital. Increasingly I was forced to employ men at higher and higher wages, with less and less qualifications. One man was excellent with the herd. He babied and pampered, soothed and polished his milking friends, but unfortunately, he never could find time to plant corn. His replacement simply loved field work, especially tractor driving, but he starved the cattle while the ground feed molded in the bin. One hand moved the milkers so slowly that

undue stress from the suction cups caused serious udder injury. Mastitis, the dread disease to all dairymen, set in and production fell to less than half.

Once through carelessness born out of desperation, I hired what seemed to be such a nice, clean-shaven man. Just twenty-four hours before he was to have moved in, an alert friend fortunately discovered my error and informed me that I had engaged a chronic drinker who became very violent when intoxicated. I was considerably more wary of the next applicant. After investigating a bit I discovered that he had just been released from the State Penitentiary, where he had served on a morals charge.

My first taste at making decisions and management proved quite unpalatable, even though I could visit Marvin at the hospital and share my problems with him.

Realistic Martha looked at the red figures in the account book and the waste caused by mismanagement. She took note of the fact that the day might come when Marvin would no longer be there to share her problems. Martha simply shook her head at the whole situation.

She had one other great concern — me. With the full responsibility of eight young children (one of these a baby), the care of an ailing husband who frequently required long hospital vigils at his bedside, the constant tension caused by fear of another stroke, plus the management and care of the farm, I was surely headed for a complete nervous and physical collapse at a time when my family needed me so desperately.

Then came the day when it seemed things couldn't possibly become worse. Marvin was taken by the most severe stroke he had ever had. While his life hung by a slim thread and doctors gravely shook their heads, suggesting that living at all was doubtful and recovery questionable, Martha made the first big decision without her husband: "The cattle and machinery must go!"

Her arguments were valid enough. There were those red figures in the account book and no replacement in sight for hired help. Marvin's brother was helping out temporarily until his college classes resumed in the fall. There was the concern for my health and Marvin's too. If Marvin did recover, it would be better if the tractors and cattle were gone. He was taking such large doses of an anticoagulant drug that even a slight bruise or a small cut could become fatal because of excessive bleeding. Adding to this danger, of course, was the unpredictability of the spells, which would make driving farm machinery extremely hazardous. Then, too, as long as the tractor stood in the shed, or the cattle in the barn, the temptation would be simply too great for Marvin. All too soon he would be doing work that was forbidden.

Realistic Martha took note of one more fact. Because of a certain amount of brain damage caused by the several strokes, Marvin no longer had the necessary mental facilities with which to make sound judgments. Both his memory of the present-day events, as well as his sense of responsibility, were seriously impaired.

Martha began arrangements for a farm auction. She simply informed her husband later.

Idealistic Mary looked on loathsomely and called her "traitor."

So Idealistic Mary and Realistic Martha worked and struggled together — each bringing her own virtues and vices. At times they complemented each other; at others they merely tolerated one another.

In one area of life Mary and Martha really clashed. So fierce was the battle at times that they nearly tore me apart. This warfare was spiritual.

Mary was so sure that if she would just hope fervently enough and pray without ceasing, that everything would turn out all right. She had ample proof for her conclusions. Many times she had seen those stickers on car bumpers and men's lapels, "Prayer Changes Things," and she had taken mental note of them. Her Bible reassured her over and over that God would hear her prayers. Paul's advice to the Thessalonians instructed her: "Rejoice evermore, pray without ceasing," and she did. Frantically she clung to the precious words from the fifth chapter of the Book of James, "Is any among you afflicted? Let him pray . . . the prayer of faith shall save the sick."

And faith? Jesus said it simply enough:. "If ye have faith as a grain of mustard seed, ye shall say unto this mountain, Remove hence to yonder place; and it shall remove; and nothing shall be impossible to you." Mary wasn't asking for a mountain to move — just for an illness to leave the man she loved. When outward appearances indicated that Marvin's health was improving, her spirits ran high and expectant.

But other days came — days when Marvin would be thrown back to the very brink of death, days when she would be forced to admit that in spite of occasional reprieves the process of regression was gradually picking up speed. At those times Mary could not hope. She couldn't even really pray. Martha would taunt her, "Where is that faith now?"

Once, in desperation, Mary cried out to a very dear friend, "There are times I just lose hope."

"Oh — you mustn't do that!" came the startled reply. It wasn't a *must* or *mustn't* — the fact was that she did, and her friend did not understand. Mary tried to hope. Martha accused her of wishful thinking. Yet both strove to find the answer.

They were not helped at all by the elderly man from the Spiritualist camp, who came knocking at the door one day.

"Join our group. Allow me to ask our leader to pray for your husband," he insisted. "Your husband will be healed if you'd join with us," he pleaded.

Mary wavered with indecision, willing to grasp at any straw in order to hold the man she loved.

Martha, fortunately, was assisted by an even older saint from her own church, who appeared on the scene just then. "Listen," he reproved, "if prayer by itself ever cured any man, this woman's husband will live. Never has this entire community been so united in prayer for anyone! If God wills it so, Mr. Kooiman will live."

Realistic Martha remembered other prayers where faith did not result in favorable answers. There was the prayer

of the Apostle Paul for removal of a thorn. The thorn remained. And the prayer of the Sinless One: "Father, if it
be thy will, may this cup pass from me." The cup did not
pass. He became my dying Savior upon the Cross.

The struggle between Mary and Martha was never
completely resolved. Each had much to learn concerning
faith and prayer.

Mary was to learn by the process of experience and
time, that prayer and faith can move mountains. Mary's
mountain was not the life or health of a loved one, but her
own insubmissive will. Her need was a will that not only
bows and accepts what her Lord sends, but includes a faith
that will accept it willingly, confident that "all things are
given for the good of those who love Him." She must be so
confident that she will look for the windows when God
has closed a door.

Later, lest Mary forget and stumble over her mountain,
Martha had these words inscribed upon the tombstone rest-.
ing there at the head of her husband's grave: "Thy Will
Be Done."

For the day came when Mary and Martha carried him to
that grave. Death intruded suddenly, unexpectedly, as un-
pretentious as the life it snatched away. Autumn was still
adorned in her Cinderella gown of scarlets, golds, and
browns — far past the sounding of the midnight's warning gong, protesting the hour she must undress and stand in
nakedness.

Then November's icy finger tore it from her. Its
breath hurled the fallen leaves about. They gathered before a tiny mound on the graveyard hill, bowing in silent
tribute to another's autumn.

Part Two

Without Daddy

CHAPTER SEVEN

"We Lost Daddy Too!"

THE FUNERAL WAS OVER. Routine life resumed itself again, and as it did, I realized that the road ahead would not be an easy one. There were so many hurdles and problems, so many fears and anxieties to face, so many decisions to make. Not only did I find myself coping with my own unfilled needs, but little David reminded me so forcefully that he had lost a daddy too and needed attention.

"Why did God have to take my daddy anyway? I want my dad. I want my dad. I hate God, Mom, I hate Him," he broke forth one noon several weeks after my husband's death.

Oddly enough this was the same child who had told his very sympathetic kindergarten teacher upon his return to school after the funeral, "Don't cry, Teacher, my dad's not dead — he's in heaven with Jesus. It's just his body in the ground." And I patted myself on the back for a job well done.

Tenderly I pressed my little one to my heart, waiting

for the sobs to subside somewhat before I began. "Davy, can you hear me?" "Do you believe that I love you? And do you love me? But once Davy, when you were cutting that box with that very sharp knife I took it away; did you know that I loved you then? I took it away because I loved you."

"Yes, but I want Daddy, I want Daddy," he interrupted.

"David, the Bible tells me that God loves us and that He does only what is good for us. I can't explain why God took Dad away, but I can believe Him when He says that He loves me." For a long moment I held him in my arms, hoping that in some small measure he would be able to identify God's love toward him through my love now, hoping that through my love he might be able to accept the love his heavenly Father held out for him.

Probably the greatest antidote to dissolving the bewilderment and hurt at the loss of a father is loving patience and understanding. A sharp rebuke at David's outburst against God at this moment would have solved nothing, except to drive his anger beneath the surface. (Hadn't the sea of depression I had just passed through been caused by rebellion on my part too?)

There are many constructive ways in which a widow can help her children, but I fear that I, wallowing in the mud of my own hurt and grief, often failed to remember or to notice the child's loss.

Not all children react with such pronounced behavior as did David, and they are the ones we so easily ignore.

I think of my littlest one, hardly three and one-half years when his daddy left so suddenly in that long black car with a door in back, never to return again. His behavior suddenly became one of extreme over-dependence upon me.

Before Marvin's death he had been an outgoing and trusting child. Everyone was his friend! Overnight he seemed to retract into forceful, anti-social behavior, even afraid to be left with his grandparents and favorite relatives. How annoying it was to find him shrieking in terror every time I left him for a few minutes. It was impossible for me to dash into a store for a single article without returning to a hysterical child. Many times I was utterly exasperated, and I met the situation head-on with a punitive impatience. It was some time before I realized that his plaintive pleas of "How long?" or "When will you get back, Mommy?" or his "Please don't go," beginning each weepy session, were in reality a frightened "Are you really coming back?" His behavior made sense when I reflected upon it. At the age of three he was too young to understand death. He only knew that his daddy disappeared quickly and did not come back. If it had happened to his father, couldn't it happen to his mother too?

In a very real sense I was also feeling his insecurity. The new role of widowhood, with all its complex problems and anxieties, was a pressing one. Then, too, at every turn following Marvin's death, I saw danger. I became afraid. I later came to realize that a small child with no father, and a disturbed, anxious mother was bound to react just as my Jerry was doing.

Because of my own incessant though unreasonable fear, I made a special trip to my lawyer to make certain that my children were well protected by a will. I also appointed a guardian. But poor Jerry could make no arrangements for his own protection — he couldn't even fathom his real fear, much less express it. Crying in terror was only a normal reaction of a small insecure child.

Like any other problem, once it is faced squarely, its solution begins rising to the surface. The course for me was to provide ample reassurance of my love and concern for him. Whenever the occasion arose, I would repeat, "Jerry, I mended your shirt because I love you," or "I made this special dessert just for you." When on occasions I found it absolutely necessary to leave him momentarily, I would repeat, "Jerry, I must leave you, but I *am* coming back, I am coming back," or, "When that big black hand on the clock gets around to that 6, I'll be here."

I also found that it really wasn't necessary to leave him as much as I thought. My trips to the grocery store, the bank, or the power and light company to pay my bill, were unquestionably slowed down by taking him along. How easy it is to save time rather than take time to love, but gradually his fears did subside. A cheerful, happy, sociable child, especially a mother's baby, is surely worth those few extra minutes.

Teen-age daughters need help and understanding too. Remorse filled my heart as the words, "Mom, we lost Daddy too!" sliced through my warped, selfish consciousness one morning, many weeks after Marvin's death.

Weeks earlier, while we were gathered at the breakfast table, I had tried to prepare the older children for a possibly adverse reaction on my part, something they might not understand. I began, "Children, you know how very much I loved your father. Going on without him will be very hard for me. Sometimes when people lose one who is very dear to them, they become very unhappy for a while. I'm unhappy now. Unhappy people say and do strange things they really don't mean and intend to do at all. Unhappy mothers often react by nagging and scolding, even

60

punishing others about them. If I begin to behave like that in the weeks and months ahead, please try to remember that I love you very much. It's probably not you I'm angry at. When I become irritable, quick-tempered, and fault-finding, please try to be understanding and find some way to remind me of what I'm doing. I don't *want* to punish you for my unhappiness and loneliness — ever!"

But I did. Many times!

They did remind me — once.

Everything had gone wrong that morning. I arrived at the barn with the purpose of milking my four cows, only to find that one of the automatic waterers in the hen house had operated automatically all right. It had kept running all night. Of course, hens don't swim, but they must investigate. "Come on ladies, this is new," I could hear them cackle to one another. All one thousand of them, it seemed, were having a grand time marching back and forth through the floating bedding, plopping up and down with pronounced steps, resembling the majorettes leading our high school band.

Hot tears stung my face as I contemplated the hours of back-breaking work involved in lifting all that wet, soggy, heavy bedding into the wheel barrow and pushing it out of the building. The only reason that the waterer could run undetected all night was that I couldn't hear the new submersible water pump, one-hundred-fifty feet down the new well I had been forced to drill. Both had meant large expenses I hadn't anticipated, all because the old well had been found to be contaminated.

Salty tears adulterated the milk as I plodded on with the morning chores. "Where was my helper anyway?" Each morning the children took turns at helping me in the barn, while the others supposedly began household duties. That morning no one showed up.

"The hen house will have to wait until after breakfast," I decided as I stalked toward the house angrily and quite out of sorts.

Breakfast was supposed to be prepared when I returned. That day no breakfast was ready, no school lunches had been packed, and no daughters were in sight!

In a fit of rage I began screaming and shouting. Hot, resentful accusations all out of proportion to the situation thundered forth in verbal avalanches. "Where was my chores-girl?" "Why isn't breakfast ready?" "You're nothing but a bunch of lazy, good-for-nothings," and more escaped my lips.

Had I looked a little more carefully I would have seen one of the distressed young ladies coming from the sewing room. She was repairing her slip — the one I had promised to mend the evening before and hadn't. Another quickly stopped ironing her blouse — the one I hadn't gotten to the day before either. (A heavy fog of despair made it so difficult to get any of my work finished those days.) My chores-girl quietly laid her algebra book aside. She had asked me the previous evening if she might do a little studying the next morning, and I had so sweetly assured her that I could manage by myself for once. But I hadn't!

I saw only the cold coffee pot, the messy kitchen table — cluttered as usual with pens, folders, books, apple cores, and cooky crumbs — and the empty lunch boxes. All the while the clock on the wall was keeping time to the parade in the hen house.

"Doesn't anyone care? Can't anyone give me a hand?

Must all this be my load alone?" I challenged, and then dashed to my bedroom. It was too much.

Then she came — Linda — quite some time later. "Please Mommy, we're sorry, please come for breakfast."

I sat dejected, unmoved, my face bowed and cupped in my hands. Tenderly she stroked my head as she uttered those cutting words, "Mama, we lost Daddy too!"

How often, after I pulled myself out of that morass of despondency, I realized with pain and regret that I had forgotten just that — my children's needs. Many times I asked, "Oh, God, why do you allow these eight precious, beautiful lives in my selfish, unworthy hands?"

Sometimes I feel that my children must be maturing more quickly than most. Perhaps through my failures they learned lessons about life they might have gained much more slowly otherwise. I felt well rewarded one evening when Linda said of her employer, "Mom, Mrs. J_____ is so irritable lately. I'm sure she must be very worried about something." She had learned a truth many adults fail to grasp in a lifetime, simply that one cannot take all external behavior at face value. Understanding the behavior of others involves an appreciation of their problems, their wounds, and their motives beneath the surface. It means averting hasty judgments.

I certainly pray that my many and obvious failures at being the perfect mother may yet be used by the Lord to teach compassion and understanding to my precious little ones.

CHAPTER EIGHT

On Making Boys into Men

*B*OYS HAVE SPECIAL NEEDS. I was especially impressed by this one evening a few months after Marvin's death, as I stepped out of our sagging station wagon.

Tears mounted in my eyes as I surveyed the damage I had done by attempting to back the car out of the garage with one flat tire. My ears rang with, "When will you remember that there is more to driving a car than filling the gas tank!" spoken more in alarm at my carelessness than in anger, by my husband just weeks before his death. I had done it again! How my husband's soul must have groaned then, knowing his days here with me were so few, and I always in too much hurry for caution.

"Call the neighbor, or Grandpa, to help," my young fatherless boys advised. (My older daughters were gone; we were about to go and get them.) I almost agreed with the boys, but remembering that this trouble might have occurred along some dark, lonely road, I determined to use this opportunity to practice meeting just such an emergency.

With an air of assurance I did not really possess, I found myself saying, "No, boys, we are fixing this ourselves." As I opened the spare tire compartment my eyes fell on Dad's old shirt and trousers, placed there for such a time as this. By the time I had slipped them on, over my good dress, the boys had already solved the intricacies of putting the jack together. With an air of adventure they helped me set it under the car bumper, and we began carefully to crank it upward, but after two pumps of the handle, the jack slipped. "Why do they make square plates to place under rounded edges?" I muttered. (I was to find out later that this jack had replaced another and that it was never meant to lift my car, but we didn't know that then.) The second try proved no better than the first, and during the third attempt not only did the jack slip, but the handle bounced back, slapping me with a sickening thud on my face and leaving an angry gash along my nose.

At the sight of their bleeding mother, the boys became thoroughly alarmed, and with frightened voices cried, "Please, Mama, call Grandpa to help." Was it some inward courage or just plain stubbornness that made me say, "Are we quitters or men?" "Remember boys," I went on, "success always comes after the last failure," and so we again tackled the task before us, this time even more carefully and with more respect for that handle. Praise God, this time we succeeded, and the rest of the work moved along quite swiftly — until with the new wheel on, we attempted to remove the jack. We all remembered that Dad had done something with the handle to reverse the jack, but no one was sure just what. We wiggled the handle up and down, but only succeeded in raising the car one notch higher each time. Finally in desperation I jerked the handle sharply upwards, and our battle was won: we were at least one notch down, and knew the secret for finishing the job. With the tension removed we all sat back and had a good laugh over our troubles, and it was not until then that the boys first realized what I was wearing. "No wonder we made it, Mom, you are wearing Dad's overalls" one of them remarked. Tenderly I folded them and placed them back in the trunk. It wasn't just the trousers that counted, I reflected, for we were no longer just a mother with two young sons — we were three men!

To mold boys into men is one of the greatest challenges, I believe, a widowed mother has. It takes courage and strength. This alone is not the full solution. Boys must also have men in their lives with which to identify themselves. The Lord has provided, in my case, a most wonderful brother-in-law, the children's uncle, who has almost literally become a second father. He is the kind of uncle who drops his fishing pole and drives into town just to invite my fatherless sons to come too, "because fishing is so good," knowing full well his fishing time will be over once my boys join his four already at shore.

He's the kind of an uncle who not only takes note of the crestfallen three-year-old back in the car, " cause his mommy thinks he's too little for fishing," but even carries him to the weedy shore and hands him a miniature pole, all the while reassuring him that he was the very reason Uncle had called in the first place. He is the uncle who is willing to make a thirty-mile round trip in fifteen-degree-below-zero weather just to hear these little boys repeat two

lines in their church Christmas program, because their own daddy can never hear them.

My boys also have Grandpa Loomans, who can keep them fascinated by the hour with his boyish pranks of yesteryear in the great northern woods.

He is a grandpa who at once bestows upon my boys all the love and pride for sons he never had, but who also requires enough respect and reverence to keep things shipshape, the way Grandpa insists they always should be. He is a man who by his own living example teaches them respect for hard work and a job well done.

Few fatherless sons are as fortunate as mine. I can never thank God enough for the help of an uncle and a grandfather whom my boys will never forget.

I have read many warnings to mothers of fatherless sons not to lean too heavily on these sons, creating a burden of responsibility too great for their young shoulders. While I recognize this possible danger, I wonder if it is not of quite some value to encourage a sense of tenderness, protection, and care toward women and girls; at least I came very much to this conclusion once when two so-called gentlemen watched, then turned around and left us while I and my little sons dug ourselves out of a huge snowdrift.

CHAPTER NINE

Speaking of Daddy

*D*ADDY CAME BACK — almost anyway.

It started at Grandma's. My little four-year-old was standing before the television set, studying our family picture as if it were the first time he had seen it. Possibly because Grandma's picture was placed at his eye level, he took notice of it. (Ours, in a much larger frame, hung high on our livingroom wall.) I was listening to him as he was pointing out each member of the group with a little, chubby finger and announcing, "Look Mama, there is me, and there is Linda, and Judy and me and you and Howie and me and —"

Suddenly he paused at the figure of Daddy, and stumbling, as if for want of words, he continued, "and there is, and there is —" Then looking almost fearfully at me, in a hushed voice he whispered, "There's my Daddy."

All through the day and the long lonely night the words, "and there is, and there's, and there's," kept echoing and re-echoing in my consciousness. Each time I heard them I kept seeing his half-fearful face. Why had my little one been so reluctant to say "my Daddy?" Did it hurt so much? Was he perhaps sparing me? When was the last time he had mentioned Daddy? or for that matter, when was the last time anyone at our house had mentioned him?

Among the hundreds of sympathy cards and letters I had received at the time of my husband's death, there was one letter which contained this message: "As time goes on you will want to speak of him often to your children." These words now rang in my consciousness as I probed for an answer. When had I last mentioned Dad to the children? The past weeks had been such dark and difficult ones, and the very thought of my husband had brought such pain and loneliness. Could it be, I wondered, that to ease the way for me my children consciously or unconsciously were avoiding talk of Daddy in my presence? I must make sure.

The occasion to find out came more quickly than I had anticipated. We were having dinner the following evening, when my kindergartener began telling us the story of "Peter Rabbit." Is there a child who does not get excited over and over again about Peter's escapades in the garden? But it was the mention of bunnies which brought a very funny incident to mind, with Daddy as the hero.

"Children," I began, "have I ever told you about the time that Daddy decided to rid our orchard of bunnies? Once when you older children were very small, we had a lovely new orchard started, with several young trees. In the fall Dad had carefully wound each little tree with fencing in order to protect them from hungry, nibbling bunnies. But that winter was no ordinary winter. The snow fell and the wind blew, and some more snow fell and the wind blew even harder, until the little apple trees were surrounded by snow drifts much higher than their wire collars. And the bunnies soon discovered the tender bark made good gnawing. Well, whenever Dad decided to take action, he never took half-way measures."

I proceeded to tell the rest of the hilarious incident. I tried to recapture for them the picture of their dad chasing through the snow in bare feet, with his shirt tails flying. The children responded with a good laugh, and then the questions began: "Mom, did this really happen?" "How old was I then?" "Did Dad really go out in bare feet?"

It wasn't long before a new kind of remembering began. "Say Mom, do you still remember when . . . ?" and, "I can still see how funny Dad looked that time we . . . ."

Yes, we were long at dinner that night. I doubt if any of us remembered what we ate though. I realized that for far too long I had been responsible for keeping a door locked, a door which should never have been closed in the first place. In a very real sense I had handed their dad back to them through the avenue of memories.

How unfair I had been. How much there was to learn in my new role — I seemed to learn so slowly. We speak often of Dad now and what a lot of joy it brings. Memories have a way of healing. Children have a right to these and should be encouraged to remember their departed father. I learned the hard way.

There are ways in which we do not speak of Dad. I have never tried to manage the children by reminding them of the punishment they might be receiving if Dad were here, nor do I feel it is right ever to curb their behavior by reminding them that Dad might be watching from up in heaven. Dad was the most devoted dad a child ever had, and we keep him that way.

CHAPTER TEN

Living Joyfully

*B*ASKETBALL? BASKETBALL? TONIGHT?
"But children, we just buried Dad last week, you
can't mean that you really want to go to a game
tonight," I protested. One look at their anxious, crestfallen
faces told me that they meant just that.

"But Mom," one of them explained, "you and Daddy
promised we would go to all the Friday night games, remember? And it is Friday night."

As if to clinch the argument, another added, "It's always so sad and droopy around here. Can't we ever have
fun anymore just 'cause Dad died?"

It was true that a few weeks earlier, when Dad had
still been here, the problem of basketball attendance had
arisen. We had then decided that we would try to make
all the Friday night games. We could neither afford all
the season's games, nor did either of us approve of late
Tuesday nights (the night on which most of the games
were scheduled). As a compromise we had settled for all
the Friday games. That was *before* Dad had left us so sud-

denly. A week after his death I wasn't ready yet for all the noise, excitement, and cheering I knew I would encounter at the game.

"Basketball so soon after Dad died?" I repeated. Then "What would people say?" slipped from my lips even before I realized that I had thought them. My hearing wasn't faulty though, and it wasn't the dejected faces of the children nearly so much as the re-echoing of those words which brought us to the game later that evening.

Long months before, when it was apparent that all too soon I would be left alone, I had decided that I would do all within my power to keep our home as nearly normal as possible after Dad left us. I had seen so many fatherless children punished unfairly by depressed mothers, mothers who seemed to die with their partners, allowing the bewildered children hardly one parent, much less two. I had also seen the frightened, anxious faces of a motherless family, when a bitter, resentful father forgot that his children still needed him. This I had vowed would not happen in my family; yet there I was, already more concerned with what others would think or say than with the well-being of my little ones.

I had started out all right, I thought. Realizing how much security the children derived from the routine and scheduled events of the day, I had begun at once to resume them. There were many of these rites at our house.

Once, in the early months of our marriage, Marvin made it quite plain (while I was dashing from table to bedroom to bathroom and then back to the table, intent on keeping an engagement, eating a bite myself and serving my husband) that from that point on our meal together was to be the important thing, and *no* other activity was to interfere.

As the family grew, this rule was strictly adhered to. Every meal, from Sunday breakfast to Saturday supper, found the entire family gathered around our old maple table. What a blessing and a joy mealtime has been and how much it did to develop family togetherness, for although the laws of attendance and promptness were rigid, the atmosphere was anything but that. With all due respect to an older generation, the philosophy that "children should be seen and not heard at the table" is one that neither of us believed in. Our table, especially the evening meal, soon after the children had returned from school, was one constant round of "Guess what?" and "You should have seen . . ." or "You can't imagine what . . .," all sandwiched between the usual "p-l-e-a-s-e pass the sugar" and "Who's holding up the gravy?"

In the process of readjustment, I really valued this family strength and oneness. Where but at a table with loved ones around can family goodwill and love be tied so beautifully into bonds of strength? What better time is there for Mom and Dad to sit back and listen to their children and gain new understanding and insight into life as it presents itself to them? For the first meal after Marvin died, I quietly gathered all nine of us about the table — we tried to eat, after our little prayer of thanks to God and a request for grace for the day, the grace I so sorely needed just then.

We were forced to maintain our regular chores too. It was good for us. The first evening after Marvin's death found us all clad in overalls, some feeding the chickens, some gathering eggs, others packing them. I was milking our four cows, while the wee ones fed their pet cats, the dog, and the baby calf. Each of us worked with the other until all the work was finished. Our spirits were not up to the usual race — "the last one to the house is the monkey" kind, in which the last one usually proved to be me.

The family institution of the "quiet hour" was re-established immediately too. This was the hour when the little ones were all scrubbed and in their pajamas. The older children dropped their schoolwork and joined in for a little snack, while Mom took all of them on *Adventures with Bill Collins,* or on a mystery with "Teddy." Sometimes we ended with a Bible story; Saturday nights we read the Sunday school lesson. Occasionally we gathered around the piano to sing. Always we ended with short evening devotions. Each child was encouraged to voice a short oral prayer all his own, inspired by a brief review of all the day's blessings or by a reminder of a pressing need on the part of someone we knew. Many weeks after Marvin's death my three-year-old would still be heard saying, ". . . and God bless Mama and Daddy," the words his departed Daddy had taught him, and I had not the heart to change. Startled, sympathetic friends came to our home that first night to console us. They found us all gathered around Mom, listening to a story and ending with our evening prayers. These friends later told me that *they* had left consoled.

Yes, I had picked up these family routines immediately upon my husband's death. I believe it was easier to do so then than it would have been to do so later. Actually these practices did more to restore me than they helped the children. It was these very institutions and customs which made it possible for me to carry on at first, even though mechanically, purely out of force of habit, moving slowly from one to the other, just performing what needed doing next. But fun — family fun — hadn't become a part of our home again. We used to have such exhilarating times together. The lovely walks and hikes in the great outdoors, the picnics, the drives. Swimming and tobogganing, each in its season. How wrapped up we became in those winter contests of checkers, caroms, and monopoly. Looking back, I realize that our home surely must have seemed drab — "droopy," my son had said. I supposed that I was as droopy and drab as their spirits.

In this connection I was facing another problem, a personal one — the wearing of black as a symbol of mourning. All through our marriage Marvin had refused to allow me to wear black. "Honey," he said once, "you look ghastly in black. It just doesn't become you. You were meant for pinks, reds, and golds — get rid of that black dress!" "That black dress" had been a beautiful two-piece wool knit of a quality I would never have been able to afford; but it had been given to me by a friend who had put on too much weight. It wasn't until I had purchased a multi-colored scarf of oranges, reds, and golds, which I deftly tucked around the neck line, that I was allowed to wear it at all. Once when I had brought up the matter of just one black dress for a very formal occasion he said, "Not even a funeral would justify black on you. If I thought you'd go around wearing black after I'm gone, I'd turn over in my grave."

I did look ghastly in black, and it depressed me, but in my community everyone wears black after a family bereavement, some for months and months — supposedly a matter of respect! For me, wearing black wasn't a matter of respect for my late husband. It was depressing — to me and to my children. Depression wasn't anything I needed, nor did my children need a despondent mother. At that

76

point I was their security and their strength. I was quite aware that they were taking their cues from me and reacting to their father's death very much as I did. I wasn't helping them much. If for no other reason than their well-being, I could not go on living by what people thought. My role right then was to be a living parent to eight bewildered youngsters.

I grabbed my coat and purse — there was just time for a mad dash to Penny's Department Store.

"Finish the chores early," I shouted as I left the house, "so we can take in the first game too."

"The game was great," the kids told me, but I doubt if they cheered louder or longer for their team than they did over my new heather-gold shift.

I doubt if anyone of us realizes how much of our lives is governed by public opinion and what people say. Society has us all pegged into certain roles, and we strive to perform them, often with little regard to the merit of our behavior. The role of widowhood is probably the most overplayed of all. Everyone has heard of the widow who grieves so long — "She is a long time getting over him; it's about time she stops feeling sorry for herself." Or the widow who masks her pain —"She surely got over him fast!" Or the widow who chooses to dress fashionably and attractively — "She must be looking for another man."

In any case the widow is expected to exhibit the outward semblances of grief and mourning after her husband passes, although the length may vary in different communities or social circles. Somehow there seems to be a notion that these little manifestations of sorrow are virtuous in themselves.

Basketball? A week after Dad died? New clothes?

Heather-gold? That evening I answered yes to those questions, perhaps somewhat impulsively, but looking back, I think the reason for my answers lay deeper than community mores and my response to the reactions of others. I suppose it all comes down to my view of death.

In this connection I am reminded of King David. He experienced a death in the family too. He had been told that because of his sin his little son would die. David was grief-stricken, so much so that his servants hesitated to bear him the news that his son was dead, for fear of what the king in his grief might do. Surprisingly, David broke the fast and asked for his clothes and food. When the startled servants inquired how this could be, he answered, "What would be the point of my fasting. Could I bring him back again? No, I shall go to him, he will not come back to me."

Isn't that just what our faith is all about? We mourn our loss — the earthly ties are so strong. But life goes on and for the Christian it is so much easier to continue, knowing that although our loved ones will never come back, some day we shall be reunited with them. Why not then return to the routine and the customary? Certainly there is no better way for a widow to help her little ones than by restoring fun and normal family activity as quickly as possible. My children insisted upon it a bit too soon, I thought, but I am glad they did.

Of course, there will be days when that reunion in heaven seems to be so very far away. There will be days of loneliness, days when we are blue and depressed, but is there any virtue living thus?

I am certain that God meant that my loved one should die — otherwise it would not have happened. Although I cannot understand God's reasoning, I am told in His Word that it is for the best. I am aware, too, that Marvin shall never come back, even though in my selfishness I might wish it so. I can believe that some day I shall go to him. What a reason for rejoicing!

Nowhere in God's Book are we instructed to live morbidly and sadly. God does not intend that his children should go on being sad and unhappy. The apostle Paul, even in the midst of severe trial, instructs us, "rejoice and again I say rejoice." In another place he writes, ". . . I have learned, in whatsoever state I am, therein to be content." I'm thankful that he included the word *learned*.

Part Three

Walking the Widow Road

That road — who can describe it?

It's the empty slippers, the vacant chair at the dining table,
the lonely space in my bed.

The lonely desolation upon returning home in the black
of night —

Unheard and unnoticed.

The twinge of pain caused by the clever words which
Sonny spoke, going by, unshared,

And the aching void at another woman's "Can I get your
sweater, Clarence?"

It's the bubble about to burst, which goes unbroken — to
tell the gay tidings to the one who cares.

It's the loss of love's need, and needing to be needed.

And the anguish and hell in the still of the night,
to reach to cover the man who's not there.

It's the sickening sensation, in a moment of fright,

With no one to comfort, no one to right.

It's the unsolved problems, worries and cares, now not
ours but mine alone.

The unaccompanied pride, hollow and empty, sitting without him on Daughter's big night.

And the forlorn faces of my four little sons, watching
a dad romp with his boys on the shore.

That road? It's all these and more —

Oh, God I've failed to describe it.

CHAPTER ELEVEN

If I Can Just Once

*I*T WAS MY SON'S BIRTHDAY. Although our family finances had never been at the "whipped-cream" level, and birthday gifts had always been either a much-needed pair of shoes, a shirt, or just a pair of boots, birthday time always brought one of Mom's special cakes as well as the right on the part of the celebrating one to choose the entire menu for the birthday supper. The day before his birthday I asked my son what he was planning for his birthday supper. Without a moment of hesitation he said, "I want roast beef with roast potatoes and carrots alongside, baked beans, and, oh, Mom, couldn't you bake us some rolls just once?"

I had always loved to cook, and encouraged by my husband's never-ending praise for my efforts, cooking had become for me a favorite art. Although my husband had always praised my meals, it was just these very foods which always brought forth a stream of appreciation. I can still hear the, "Children, we have the best mom!" over my pies and rolls, an "aren't we glad we married her!" over a

roast beef, and a "boys, when you get married make sure you get a cook like that," while he helped himself to another helping of baked beans. So when my young son asked for these very foods my heart wanted to scream, "Child, that's not fair, I can't make these foods — these belonged to your dad!" With panic hidden in my breast, I managed a weak, "So that's what you want for your birthday."

I was quite aware that I had avoided these foods, in fact, practically avoided cooking at all. With my husband no longer there to cook for, the special efforts at the kitchen range had lost all meaning. My meals these last several weeks had been as uninspired as my luncheons when I expected no one but myself. In all honesty I realized that my children had neither died, nor had their appetites vanished, and I really should not have been surprised to find out that they enjoy food as their dad did. It was just that it seemed almost sacriligious to prepare these, his favorites, when he could no longer eat them.

The whole day was darkened by a cloud of depression. I went through the motions of preparing these foods more out of habit than with thought. Surprisingly enough the rolls turned out quite well, in spite of the lack of tenderness and devotion with which I usually handled them.

Two thoughts carried me through the hours, one a phrase I remembered from the Bible, "I can do all things through Him who strengtheneth me. . . ." I asked, "All things Lord, even this?" And the Lord had answered "ALL things!"

Then there had been the letter from an old widowed aunt. At the time of bereavement she had written, "Gladys, in the future you will find many occasions in which you will want to say, "I can't." There is little room for any "can'ts" in a widow's life. Please let me assure you of one thing: the first time is always the hardest." How many times I repeated that to myself! The first time — there have been so many first times: the first church service alone, the first public meeting without him, the first serious discipline measure toward a naughty child, the first drive to our favorite scenic spot without Dad — oh so many firsts, and how difficult they were! But how true, too, that although the second time may not have been easy, "the first is always the hardest."

As the little voices blended in the "Happy Birthday" song, my lips joined in while my ears kept listening for "Aren't we glad we married Mom!" and my heart kept repeating, "I can do all things. . . ." and "The first time is always the hardest."

There was one especially painful first — the first time

I had to determine my new status. Two little boxes, *single* and *married,* presented themselves on a registration form that I was filling out for an evening college course.

Instinctively I started checking the box labeled *married.* Then my pencil paused in mid-air. Was I married? With no husband? I glanced at the only other alternative, and even as I did the diamonds from my wedding ring sparkled, reflecting light from the ceiling above. A wedding band — eight children at home. If I wasn't married, I certainly didn't feel single!

My hands became clammy and my forehead moist as I nervously contemplated my dilemma. I left it temporarily and began filling in other bits of necessary information: social security number, age, previous education, and former schools; but even as I did, I could not forget those two blocks behind question number five, still unchecked.

Finally in desperation I solved the problem by printing that most despicable five-letter word, *widow* (with all its stereotyped connotations), beneath the *married* box. That was the first time I even admitted to that much — *widow.*

"You great big blundering fool," I chided myself as I left the building. "You, with enough credit hours to call yourself a college senior, enrolling in a social-psychology course yet, and you don't know if you're married or single!"

Perhaps the office clerk had little difficulty with this silly widow, as she sat there reducing all my past and present into black and white, to numerals, dashes, and digits, but I seriously doubt if the computer with all its mechanical skill and intricacies really ever will quite catch me.

CHAPTER TWELVE

Loved and Lost

*T*HAT DREAM CAME BACK LAST NIGHT — it doesn't visit me as frequently — but it hasn't changed.

The dream begins with a voice (Marvin's voice) calling softly. I turn, surprised to find that he is so near. With his arms stretched out to embrace me, I move toward him. I feel his strong arms clutching me tightly, his lips pressed to mine. Always I whisper, "Oh, darling, Why have you been so long?"

Then I awaken. It is dawn, and he has disappeared. My pillow and face are wet from tears; I did not know I was crying. The dream is always the same. It is so real that I can only stare at the empty space in the bed beside me. He was so near. He was just here. I heard his voice — yet the dawn in its solemn grayness announces that it was just a dream. Just a dream, but not an ordinary kind of dream. This dream repeats itself and never ends. It is without hope, one that can never come true. I sigh knowing that today will be a heavy day, a heavy, aching day — my whole body and heart aching for his presence, aching for his voice, aching for his love. The lovely dream becomes a tormentor, torturing me by the memory of other nights when it wasn't a dream.

Conscious tears begin. I ask, "Why, God, did you give me the bliss of love — that beautiful relationship between a husband and wife — only to take it away so quickly? Wouldn't it have been better never to have loved at all, than to have loved and lost?"

I am quick to admit that love surely developed and enriched my life. It taught me patience, tolerance, forbearance, and forgiveness. It brought me a home, a family, meaning and fulfillment. But life would be so much easier now if I had never known the joy, the richness, and the ecstasy of that most meaningful relationship on earth — physical love. Our love had been so rich and so satisfying. Learning to live day after day without it is not easy. The dream re-occurring time after time only served to make it more difficult.

The attempt to sustain loss bravely, and the battle to overcome deprivation is never likely to be victorious without effort on one's part to make it so. Self-discipline and positive, constructive attitudes are both necessary.

Self-acceptance, as we are, is one such attitude. Frequently in the area of sexual expression one who has lost a marriage partner acquires guilt feelings concerning the desire for and the urgency of the physical relationship which has been swept away. To fail to admit to ourselves that we crave this expression of love is less than honest; yet to feel guilty about these sensations is to become our own stumbling block. It is well to remember that God instituted marriage and that He imbued men and women with the natural instinct of physical love. This drive not only perpetuates the human race, but also serves the purpose of fanning the flame of love and devotion, keeping it burning warmly and brilliantly. If my physician were to demand that I strike all sweets and pastries from my diet, I would do all I could to abstain from using them; however, I am sure that I would not stop drooling over berry pies and cream puffs in my baker's window. It is also foolish to expect that when a lover dies one should cease to crave for the physical diet of love he or she once enjoyed. The right or the wrong of the matter lies with the way in which we cope with the problem, not in the feelings themselves. For the young widow, temptation is very great. It is not only created by the drive from within but also by the popular attitude of so many men who think the widow is an easy mark.

For those of us who love our Lord (and ourselves), there is really only one solution: total abstinence, both in mind and body. Many times God heard and answered my prayer, "Oh God, don't let me do anything foolish!" He was always there to help.

A second positive attitude I gained from my basic psychology and physiology studies — I'm so glad for the formal education I received. Quite contrary to popular belief, I learned that sexual activity is not necessary for a perfectly normal and healthy body and mind. Malicious advertising has sold our nation on the opposite thinking. Sex has been exploited all out of proportion to its actual place in life, and it is being used to sell everything from cars to deodorant creams, from mouth washes to "the pill", from hair dye to movie tickets. In the process, sex has been cheapened to mere physical appetite. It has lost much of the beauty for which it was intended, that of enriching a deep and abiding love and strengthening the marriage tie. Sexual activity is not necessary for happy, joyful living. Just as in a reducing diet, the enjoyment of other good foods eventually replaces the desire for fine pastries and dulls their luster, so too in love life one can find other rewarding activities to replace the loss. God created me a woman; I do not pretend that all natural desire will be erased, but time, total abstinence, and new life-interests all serve to blunt the edge of need or desire. The thwarted emotion does subside.

Careful observation taught me too, that the pressing urgency often came in cycles, very strong at times, and other times less so, but regulated very closely by normal monthly body functions. In moments of intense feelings it is a great help to remember that in a few days the pressure will not be as great.

Some of the helps I found to diminish the frustration were hard physical work and activity. Digging in the garden, washing windows, painting my house, long walks, and strenuous sports all had their turns. Physical exhaustion often relaxes emotional disturbance. Reading was another outlet which helped control strong feelings; on particularly lonely nights I often read into early morning hours.

New social activities, especially those in which I felt I was contributing something toward life, such as my Sunday class with young people, substitute teaching, and my writing. Other activities, such as night classes, Bible study, and my writer's club also helped to eliminate the problem. Engaging in these types of activities is not difficult for me because of my built-in baby-sitters. Widows of very young children would find this more difficult; yet it is important to find emotional outlets. One evening as a nursing aid, a few hours at the Red Cross center, a Sunday school class, and a night at the local Y each week are just a few of the possibilities. Their healing power may well be worth the price of a baby sitter. To think positively and to take positive steps as well are of prime importance in overcoming deprivation and maintaining self-respect.

CHAPTER THIRTEEN

Nearsighted Vision

A LITTLE CHILD SHALL LEAD THEM.
I was reminded of that truth again one evening as we were traveling along the highway, going for a visit to a friend. We were traveling toward the setting sun. It was my little son who exclaimed, "Mama, look at the beautiful sky. What makes it like that?"

The heavens were so lovely! Why hadn't I seen them? The puffs of clouds were of such a vivid blue, all edged and interlaced with strips of brilliant orange-gold sunlight. It reminded me of Grandma's patchwork quilts.

"Those dark spots are clouds, Davy, and the setting sun is peeking out and around each little puff."

It was then that he spoke those memorable words, "Mama, doesn't all that bright light just make you think of heaven?"

Oh, the shame of it! While David was beholding the heavens, my vision was glued to this earth. All I could see were the bumps in the road. I viewed with envy a lady's new house, and noticed another's not-so-white bedsheets on the line. It wasn't until after David had pointed out the celestial beauties that I saw them too, but by then David was seeing heaven and God, leaving me far behind.

Ironically enough, it was I, his mother, who had answered all those questions concerning heaven: "Mama, what is heaven like?" "Where is it?" "Can Daddy see us from there?" "Will he know me when I get there?"

A little child has endless curiosity concerning spiritual and heavenly things. It was I who had patiently tried to answer these questions, but it was for my little one to catch the vision and hold it in his simple, trusting faith.

All of us are traveling the westward road of life, toward a setting sun. Some of us must travel that road in loneliness and in disappointment. How often we plod on seeing only the bumps and holes of life, envying what others have, judging where we need not judge. How much smoother that road could be if only we would hold our sight on the "Eternal Sun" and heaven with God.

But at least I was conscious of the upward look again!

Many sad months had passed when I had not looked up at all, when all was bleak and empty. It culminated about the time of my first wedding anniversary date after Marvin's death. There were many difficult days, birthdays (especially his birthday), Christmas, New Year's Eve (that one hurts too), but it is the wedding anniversary day, the day that belonged so exclusively to the two of us, that was nearly unbearable.

My mother, sensing that the day would be painful, had called to tell me she was coming to spend the day, "to help sew and mend some," she had said. Already before she arrived I had plunged my face into cold water

95

and used make-up to cover the traces of the early morning tears which I couldn't hold back. I knew that I wasn't fooling her, but somehow I managed to keep up my end of the running conversation, hoping the tears didn't show too much in my voice. I managed to withhold them from my eyes until after she left, and then they began anew.

"Perhaps if I rest a bit I'll feel better," I told myself. I was tired. In fact, I hadn't slept well for several nights — too tense and frightened by that date I wanted to ignore, but which I knew for a certainty I would not be able to forget.

Rest would not come. Lying there, I could only see darkness and despair. The six months that Marvin had been gone seemed like an eternity already. The throbbing, pressing ache, the loneliness and sense of loss were overwhelming. And there was the neverness — a new concept to me. I had often thought of the earthly "forever" in relation to time. There is the "forever" of marriage, for instance. I suppose in unhappy marriages this seems unending, but always there remains at least a hope for a better tomorrow. I was cast into "never, never land." "Never" is a long time. The pressing consciousness of "never" developed as time went on. Never his smile? Never. Never his voice? Never. Never his caress, never his footstep to be heard again approaching the kitchen door? Never. Many, many nevers presented themselves . . . the gnawing, relentless desolation of never land.

Finally, when I felt I could stand it no longer, I slipped from the house, slid behind the wheel of our station wagon, and without a clearly-designed destination in mind, ended where I had so often during that time of distress — at his grave.

96

I had been behaving somewhat as I had the many times when Marvin had been in the University Hospital, a distance of some fifty miles from my home. There were times when he was so desperately ill that leaving his bedside was unthinkable. On one occasion I was near him for ten days without coming home. There were other times though, when he was at the hospital merely for observation and routine checkups. Then there was really no need of my being there with him; in fact, my little ones were in more actual need of my presence than he was. But the restlessness would begin to gnaw; an indescribable anxiety would press down upon me, until in desperation I would travel the road back to him. Soon, all too soon, I would return home, only to have the same process repeated again. I was repeating the pattern now, except this time I did not find him — only a green mound of dirt — his grave.

Readers may find this behavior strange, and it was (I shall never again judge the actions of anyone in grief), but as a matter of fact, I did find some measure of peace and restoration there at his grave. Perhaps this was due in part to the very beauty of the cemetery itself. It is such a beautiful spot, a place of rolling hills, a few quite steep. Many beautiful trees have been preserved; new ones had been planted so that the cemetery resembles a park as lovely as any in scenic Wisconsin. A lazy river flows softly along two sides, to the sharp edge of a waterfall nearby. Graceful willows and stately pines line the river all the way. Then, too, somewhere in my confused mind, because my eyes were still so closely bent to the physical, I actually felt close and near to my lost love there.

Inevitably, as in the hospital days, I had to return home. Then all the relentless emptiness, loneliness, and hopelessness began anew. But my first anniversary alone! I shrank at the thought of the years and years yet to come of the same!

I was headed into the greatest surge of despair and depression that I have ever known — days which I shudder to recall — days when there was no God, no hope, only dread and a restlessness which could not be dispelled. Through those days there was only one prayer, if it could be called that, "Oh, God, don't let me do anything foolish." Only God knows how near I came to doing just that!

It is with extreme pain that I bring back those days to memory — some of the moments lost to mind even as I was lost in the fog of despair. There were the questionings: "Why, God, why did You take him? Why not a worthless father, a drunk, or one who did not care for his family?"

Accompanying the questionings was the continual chant which ran through my mind, "I can't, I can't," each time a little hurdle had to be met. Anger and resentment filled my soul. I was cross with my little ones and cross with myself. Even the most insignificant decisions became too great for me. Doubts haunted me. Perhaps if I . . . if only I . . ." (as if somehow I could have prevented his death!). I began to hate those whom I felt had let me down; a stirring of envy filled me as I saw other couples walking hand in hand.

And there was no peace!

A restlessness began haunting me. I found myself moving from one thing to another in a meaningless morass, my whole being pacing back and forth like a caged animal. What an excellent target for Satan's darts — and he threw them well. Darts of hate, envy, temptation, and a desire to escape from it all. I who had never had a drink nor entered a tavern had an urge to get drunk; I who had always loved life, was now groping for ways of self-destruction.

Then there were the tears — tears shed all night, more in resentment than from actual loneliness. I was wallowing in the mud of self-pity.

And there was no God; nor was there any good!

Two episodes had to take place before I was to find the peace and the joy I was seeking. The peace in my soul could only come after I was brought to a complete submission to God's will; the joy came once again after my eyes were turned upward toward eternity — everlasting life with Him.

It began with God's Word. Carelessly, in the performance of family devotions, I had paged through the Bible and began reading Psalm 66. The Word these days held little pleasure for me. Where was God? He seemed so far from me. Then it was almost with a feeling of disgust that I passed the psalmist's words: "Shout joyfully to God, all the earth." I was a far cry from shouting joyfully!

Then the following words presented themselves: "Let not the rebellious exalt themselves." The pointing finger of a guilty conscience stabbed straight into my soul. Was this why I couldn't find God? I, who had always exalted the mind, the reason, the rational, was I trying to tell God He didn't make sense? Little I, judging the very One who turned the sea into dry ground, whose eyes observe the nations? Was I exalting myself?

Once again I recognized the old man in me. Giving my heart to the Lord, believing that I was His child — these were not so hard. But that stubborn will of mine — to will His will for me, to completely submit to His ways when they did not suit mine — that was something else again. How well Satan knew my weakness and what a good job he had done.

But Satan's power is bound. It was with a far lighter heart that I could read now: "Bless our God who keeps our soul in life, Who does not allow our foot to be moved." Thank God He does not.

This submission and its natural result, reconciliation with God, brought the rest and peace that I had yearned for. It was still to be quite some time before the third dimension of real faith, joy — real, living, unmasked joy — was to be found. My nearsighted vision was simply inadequate faith, and my faith was inadequate to the need. I had given my life to the Lord many years before; my church made sure that I knew my catechism well. All through my life I had heard excellent messages concerning the Christian's joy — the bliss of eternity. In my mind I knew these things, yet if I ever thought of heaven at all, it was only in a vague, impersonal way. This earthly existence gives us so much to think about.

As a matter of fact, I rarely thought of death either — until that early Monday morning when I witnessed life slowly slipping away; death stealing in so swiftly with its ghastly gray pallor and its swollen puffiness. Somehow, after the ambulance left so quietly, I was able to go to the children and say, "Yes, Daddy died, but he is in heaven already. All we have left there is his tired old shell which we will be bringing away soon."

Later when the morticians finished their fine art, and told us that we could see "him," it was not a dead shell I saw! "He" looked so well — so alive — so handsome all dressed in his Sunday suit. Why, "he" was just sleeping there on lovely soft beige satin. All suggestion of death was carefully erased. People came in rows to see "him." I saw "him" carried away and left there in the cemetery. My heart was buried there beside "him."

Why at death do we put so much emphasis on the body? Why are we, who call ourselves Christians, chained and locked to rituals and traditions that have their origin in pagan rites carried out so carefully to appease the dead man's spirits? I have been told that when death struck a new Christian convert in Nigeria, the bereaved husband quietly carried his wife to a shallow grave, and then invited the fellow Christians to gather with him there later in the evening — to sing praises to God! How far we Christians of an advanced culture lag behind in grasping the true meaning of death. I "head-knew" that Marvin was not there in the grave, that he was reigning with his Lord, but my heart kept wandering back — back to the grave.

There were times when I was brought up short. Once when I took the children to the grave site and showed them where Daddy was buried, one bewildered little boy asked, "But I thought you said that Daddy was in heaven?"

"Of course Daddy's in heaven, darling, this is just where his body is buried."

My heart cried, "He's here, he's here!" I came back and I came back — always leaving so empty and lost. Month after month, season after season — the Christmas message, followed by that of Easter, then Ascension Day services — but through them all I failed to gain the upward look. The second Christmas and Easter still found me looking down.

Then one lovely spring day as I sat there at his grave again, once more longing so very much for just a few moments with him, words began racing through my mind. They were words which I had heard so often — had even taught my first graders once many years before — words which could have brought me so much joy, had I remembered them.

"He is not here, He is risen." These were the words spoken of Christ that first Easter, by the angel to the women who came to the tomb to find a dead Jesus. It was all so clear now. Because He lived, we live. . . . Marvin was living! "Marvin is not here, He is living," rang through my consciousness. The beauty of that truth sang within me. I do not claim any special revelation, but I know God was there; He was simply not allowing my foot to slip.

Once again I began looking up — not every day, not faithfully — that takes faith and practice — but life again became a joyful thing. My walk, although it still was painful without my beloved husband, became meaningful. Because Marvin is *not* here — here in the grave — I can look ahead and know that some day I shall go to him.

No, my foot had not been allowed to slip — even as I faltered. There were still dark days when the loneliness seemed so cruel and hard. Days of depression too. For the benefit of these days I placed a list inside my cupboard door. It looked like this:

1. Read Psalm 66 again
2. Pray awhile
3. DO SOMETHING
   —write a friend
   —read a book
   —bake bread
   —go shopping

102

   —go fishing with the boys

   —call on a lonely person

   —anything — only DO SOMETHING

4. See your doctor

   Depression is DANGEROUS

   Caution — BEGIN REMEDY AT ONCE!

Anyone who has not passed through the inertia of depression will not realize how difficult it is to follow item 3. But the first three measures did take care of many of those days. With the help of God and faith in Him we can do much for ourselves. At times depression becomes too great; then we must recognize that outside help is necessary. A quiet talk with an impersonal doctor helped me through many such occasions. Pastors are also always so glad to listen. Both will likely recommend further psychological treatment if they feel it is important.

One must also remember that the physical and mental are closely intertwined. Fatigue can be the result as well as the instigator of depression. The shock of death in the family, the funeral rites, and the long hours of greeting sympathizing friends all take their toll on the human body. After severe shock, appetites often vanish; sleep is restless and broken, and our bodies begin to wear down. Not infrequently, when these physical disorders disappear, depression also moves along. It is unfair to ourselves as well as to our children to neglect our physical health.

Ancient Greeks stressed "healthy minds and healthy bodies." I would add the third ingredient — healthy spiritual hearts. These three combined can only make for joyful living.

CHAPTER FOURTEEN

I Was a Stranger

ONE OF THE GREATEST NEEDS OF A WIDOW is friends — people who care. Tizzie, with all her crazy idiosyncrasies, made it clearly evident that there are still many people in this world who are concerned for the widow and glad to help her in any kind of emergency.

Tizzie was our old family station wagon, well named by the children, because, as they observed, "That's the state she always keeps us in." She never had any of the common ailments of automobiles; instead she always managed to get the kind other cars and mechanics knew little about or never expected a three-year-old car to come down with. Tizzie never complained when it was cold, but she disliked rainy weather. Even just damp air made her erratic and stubborn, unwilling to listen to the summons of the starter. At times she choked and coughed until she finally gave in, but usually it was only after her spark plugs had been carefully wiped off and her insides warmed and dried by an electric heat lamp or a small fan-type heater we kept handy. The extra fifteen or twenty minutes we spent coaxing her were usually those we couldn't afford to lose.

Once she lost all her supporting rods underneath her radiator and just waited for the day that I would try climbing a steep hill. Tizzie was weeping badly after the radiator fell forward into the fan. Judging by the noise she made, the pain must have been excruciating as the blades deeply embedded themselves into the radiator network.

The day she really left us down (and at the same time taught me a good lesson or two) was an unseasonably hot Sunday afternoon in mid-April. We were 350 miles from home. The reason for the trip had been a most unhappy one — a funeral in southwestern Minnesota for Marvin's brother, who had passed away suddenly. It was difficult to accept the fact of another widow and four more fatherless children, so close upon the heels of my own loss. Added to the death of another brother several years earlier, there were now sixteen of these children in one family.

I wouldn't have taken the children, except that this trip would certainly cancel the summer visit with their aunts and uncles and cousins, which I had promised them months before. Financing one, much less two, trips was already a big obstacle.

In all our life together, Marvin and I had never planned Sunday trips. Sunday was our day of rest and worship, and we sought to instill this concept in our children. On the other hand, we never consciously allowed them to miss school either. Since the long trip plus the day of the funeral already necessitated Thursday and Friday out of school, I felt we simply had to be back on Monday. I soothed my conscience and those of the children, who incidentally had become extremely critical of any endeavor on my part to go countrariwise to their dad's former concepts of good and bad, right or wrong, by first attending church services on Sunday morning. We bid farewell to my hostess sister-in-law early Sunday noon, after a hasty lunch.

Any widow who decides to travel in the Midwest on a sleepy Sunday afternoon with six young children ought to have her head examined. I discovered that too late.

Tizzie had begun to give us some concern already on the trip down. We were loaded very heavily, bucking early spring winds, and I decided that it was only natural that she heated up easily when we drove fast, and she used more water than usual. The day of the funeral, a very wet, damp day, she absolutely refused to start. At a nearby garage, the mechanics decided she needed new points and installed them, assuring me that this was the cause of all our trouble. "Tizzie could have used a few pointers instead," I decided later, when she broke down completely on our homeward trip. Three hundred and fifty miles from home her rebellion erupted in a boiling gush from the radiator. Fortunately we were just rolling into a small town and up to a garage which was open for business. Shaking his head and waving his arms helplessly, the attendant explained that he was not a mechanic. "We only service, not fix, cars on Sunday," he explained with an obvious speech impediment.

Frantically I explained that I was a widow, alone with six children and that I had to have help.

Reluctantly he called to the homes of several mechanics and finally found one of them at home who would come and see what he could do. After three hours of testing, lis-

tening, watching, starting and stopping the motor, he told me that the difficulty was most likely either a cracked block or a leaky head gasket. There was little he could do since not a single auto parts store would open until the next morning. His only recourse, mixed with some hesitation, was to pour two types of stop-leak fluid into the radiator. "Keep your fingers crossed," he suggested, and then admonished us to fill our empty jugs and thermos bottles with water — "just in case."

Although Tizzie behaved beautifully at the garage, with her motor running over thirty minutes before we ventured back on the highway, we were less than ten miles down the road when she began her explosive bursts again. After the puffing, rolling steam subsided a bit, my sister (she came along to help me drive) and I added six quarts of water, our entire supply, to the radiator, only to see Tizzie swallow it in one big gulp. We watched it disappear before our very eyes. Slowly we limped into the next town, Tizzie bubbling and rebelling all the way. We stopped at the first open gas station along the highway.

I'm not sure how the attendant sized up Tizzie, but after I frantically explained that the mechanic in the last town had concluded that we must have either a *blown* block or a *cracked* gasket, he must have deduced that I had a few loose gears floating around. "Lady, there isn't a single garage open in this whole town on Sunday," he explained. "Better you get some rooms and stay overnight."

My spirits sank to rock bottom as my thoughts centered on my billfold. Two previous garage bills had already eaten away most of the extra cash I had taken in case of emergencies. Mentally I calculated the cost of rooms for eight, additional food, and still another garage bill. Emily's

108

dry remark popped out just then: "I just knew we shouldn't have traveled on Sunday. This is our punishment for sure." It did little to help matters.

We needn't have bothered to call concerning room rates at all three motels listed in the yellow pages of the telephone directory, for when we all piled back into the car to go to the one which promised to be the most reasonable, Tizzie flatly refused to budge. Even if we had been able to go, the cost for eight was prohibitive, so we decided to put down the car seats, which could be laid flat, and allow four of the children to sleep in Tizzie for the night, on the air mattresses we had packed with our luggage. The car's unwillingness to budge made this arrangement dubious too, since we would not be able to have it parked right outside our motel door. Fortunately there was a good motel about a block uphill from where we were stranded, and four of us trudged there with heavy loads of luggage.

The motel owner listened sympathetically to our story, and although he did charge us his regular rate for four, he quickly offered extra sleeping facilities for "those poor kids back there in the car" at the unheard of rate of one dollar!

Upon inquiry we found that if we hurried, we could make the seven o'clock evening services at a local Baptist church. This involved another long climb up the steep incline, lugging the suitcases containing our dress clothes, but after the hectic day we all felt like we could use church services. In our family, humor has a way of leaking out in spite of dire circumstances. As the walk would be a long one, we decided to wear our tennis shoes and carry our heels until we approached the church. We did feel a bit foolish switching them at the street corner, using the

109

lamp post or each other to prop us while one foot was lifted in mid air. Once along the way, Marilyn who was at the early-teen age, where one simply must never appear conspicuous, suggested that we must certainly appear a peculiar lot, all walking together "in one lump" down the street.

"At least we're witnessing" came the prompt reply from one of the children at the head of the rank.

My family shall never forget the warmth and kindness with which we were greeted in that little church. Officers quickly introduced themselves and sought out our story.

The Sunday school director spoke words of reassurance and spiritual comfort when he discovered that I had lost my husband and now a dear brother-in-law. The pastor's message was simple, but filled with the love of a Savior — his talk to me later could only be described as tender and compassionate. Two families, each lacking car space for our entire family, insisted on taking half of us back to our motel. One businessman member handed me his calling card, and begged me to call on him if we lacked anything at all. It was good to sing and pray and converse with these fine Christians in spite of the fact that their services were far less formal than those we were accustomed to. Each of us left them feeling clean and whole and refreshed.

"Mommy, if we hadn't traveled today, on Sunday, would all this mess have happened?" asked Howard later at our evening devotions back in our motel rooms. I had been expecting some form of this question sooner or later and had been contemplating an answer.

"Let's look at it like this," I began. "Tizzie was not in any shape for the trip. I think she would have broken down on Monday as well as Sunday, but no one should ever do things they feel are wrong. We put school and education before God and our conscience. This was very wrong. Then too," I went on, "if we had waited until tomorrow we would have gotten expert help immediately and our delay would not have been nearly as long or expensive. Perhaps there was a special reason that all of this happened. Any experience is valuable if we learn from it, and I'm learning a lot of things."

"Like Christians in other churches, huh, Mom?"

"Like Christians in other churches, son, and kindness and love."

The remainder of the trip did *not* run smoothly! We called home to my parents on Sunday afternoon to have them make arrangements for retaining the services of the chores-boy for one more day, but we were determined to get home somehow on Monday. It was late that afternoon and my check book another sixty dollars slimmer before we were back on the road, with 350 miles still before us.

Ten minutes out of the little town, Tizzie was right back to her old tricks. Tears of frustration began tumbling down my cheeks. This time Emily saved the day: Cupping her hands to resemble a telephone call, she announced, "Grandma, we got ten miles further today!"

"Children, we're going to crawl every inch nearer home that we possibly can," I announced with grim determination. "Keep hoping that the motor doesn't stop; we'll keep filling the radiator." We did just that. At the next gas station we had the radiator filled and I purchased a five-gallon gasoline can, which we filled with water, and a kitchen funnel. From there on, we stopped at every station which was open for service, to add water. When the stops were too far apart, we hauled out the five-gallon can which we refilled at every opportunity. Indeed, we traveled by inches, but home never looked sweeter or dearer in the early morning hours.

Frequently I've heard complaints that the widow is common prey of unscrupulous business people, salesmen and dealers — that she's always being taken advantage of. The trip with Tizzie did much to reassure me of the milk of human kindness — for widows too! How else could one account for the helpfulness of the first mechanic back in Fremont, who left his Sunday dinner and T.V. baseball game to help a distressed widow? Then there was the owner of the motel in Blue Earth who arranged extra sleeping facilities for four grateful youngsters for a pittance, who looked aside as we ate sandwiches in a room where food was prohibited, and then allowed six children to remain in rooms until late afternoon, in spite of signs which insisted that occupants vacate by noon. "I'd never turn you out in this cold. (A violent storm the night before had ushered in severe cold and forty to fifty mile-an-hour winds.) "Stay put until that car is fixed," he insisted. How could I ever express the gratitude I felt toward the second mechanic to work on Tizzie at the Blue Earth garage, a young man just out of high school, who willingly forfeited his lunch hour in order to help that "widow and her kids get back on the road." Our hearts are still warmed as we remember the proprietor of the roadstand who made us delicious cheeseburgers, in spite of the fact that she wasn't really open for business, inviting us into her warm kitchen in order to escape the cold. All this, plus the hospitality we received at the church, for absolute strangers. I was a stranger, but they took me in.

112

CHAPTER FIFTEEN

Who Takes Advantage of the Widow?

IN MY OWN HOMETOWN I am *not* a stranger. Here, too, I have found countless friends who constantly make my road easier, because of the very fact that I *am* a widow. Included in the long list would be the kind lawyer who unraveled all the early financial and legal red tape of widowhood for me, and surely the shoe man who again and again rings up $4.95 on his cash register for a pair of shoes I selected, pressing two quarters of change into my fist for the $5 bill I just handed him. Often he finds a pair of cheaper shoes for a needy son from an odd lot he bought up at a closeout sale, or otherwise finds a pair that he planned to put on sale the next day anyway. There is my regular garage mechanic who cares for my car as if it were his own — who tells me when it needs a new oil filter, a grease job, or a radiator hose and would never think of taking advantage of my ignorance concerning automobiles. The friendly hardware man always maintains his smile, even when I seek more advice than merchandise. He not only is willing to take the time to dem-

113

onstrate how to replace a worn washer in a faucet, but insists I bring the faucet in, and he fixes it for the price of a small rubber disc. Nor does he lose his smile or patience when I ask the difference between a fly and a casting reel, or bring in a water hose needing a new end fitting. In my own town I have often received credit for months on end, without a single pressure for payment, because proprietors from local business places know and care that I am alone with a family. That's how my home town takes advantage of the widow!

What would I ever have done without my fine neighbors — neighbors who cheerfully offered help with farm jobs, who came running when Lucy, my large holstein, draped herself (feet dangling on both sides) over the Dutch barn door, in her enthusiasm to get out before it was open; who were at hand to help Reddy when she had calving difficulties; who pitched in to help install automatic chicken waterers when hens arrived ten days earlier than expected; or who came out with tractors on a cold, wet night when I carelessly drove off the driveway curb and got stuck in the ditch.

Nor can I forget to mention the help I've received from my family, help with decisions and farm problems, mending fences, and remodeling barns.

My church, too, stood by to help in emergencies. There have been offers of financial help on several occasions. Once it took a large collection to help defray medical bills. When I was bedridden for several months due to an old back injury, church societies brought in hot meals and baked goods for my family day after day.

Both the stranger and residents of my hometown have proven time and again to be this widow's friend — always

114

willing to give a hand in emergencies. Actually I have experienced very few incidents with the take-advantage-of-a-widow kind of dealer anywhere, but then I discovered that I do have three excellent safeguards protecting me from ruthless and high-pressured sales people.

First of all there is Chuck, my huge, watchful husky. Chucky seems to have an uncanny ability to judge character. Many a salesman, after encountering Chuck's formidable inspection, has suddenly decided that he didn't really have to stop anyway. Should such a one yet pass the dog's scrutiny, I have a second valuable protection — no money! Loan sharks, confidence men, and ruthless dealers simply aren't interested in *poor* widows.

One salesman reminded me of an even greater protection I own, should these measures fail. Chuck was dubious about him from the beginning, and was obviously less impressed by all his charm and gracious manner than I.

Upon looking back later, I realized that my line of "no money" was rightfully misjudged on his part. My lovely second-hand Buick which I had purchased to replace Tizzie, all polished and shiny, must have appeared quite luxurious standing in my drive. This "poor" widow, dressed in nylons and heels and a becoming suit, was preparing a fine beef roast for dinner. He had no way of knowing that I had just returned from an interview for a part-time job, and because I was pressed for time, had neglected to change into my usual house clothes. Even my house and furniture must have appeared a bit finer than usual, all polished and waxed for late evening guests.

Somehow, in the middle of his sales campaign for some marvelous package-insurance program he had to offer, he learned that I was a widow. His interest began in earnest. I met with the usual and by now familiar expressions of concern, followed by sympathetic phrases of flattery — "Such a pity" — I was "still so young and so nice looking too." Before long followed the sad story of his own non-understanding wife at home — until I wasn't quite sure if the product he was selling was in his brief case or whether it was the one wrapped in the shapeless blue surge he was wearing. Nor was I overly concerned. Chuck's watchful eye and pointed ears belied the relaxed and sleepy pose he was pretending. He had already given me one quizzical glance and I was sure that he understood my wink which said, "Just relax, give him a little more rope with which to hang himself," for already I could hear the distant roaring motors of the school bus as it left the neighbors' house down the road.

Then the thundering avalanche struck — one, two, three bodies burst through the kitchen door directly behind his back, as lunch buckets whizzed along the counter top, and school books and band instruments thumped upon the kitchen table, each child trying to relate all the day's exciting events at the same time. On and on they came — five, six, seven, eight, nine. Ironically, that afternoon two nieces came along too for dinner and an evening of play.

As the last of the procession swarmed past he finally mastered his speechless throat and uttered, "Are all these kids yours?"

"Oh, yes," I assured him, "and don't you think I have a lovely family?"

With sudden alarm and earnest study of his wrist watch he remembered an important appointment for which he was already late. With sincere apologies for having taken so much of my time, he backed out, his eyes still wide

116

with obvious horror. Brand new overshoes, which he forgot in his haste, are still awaiting his return. Somehow I feel that one of these days they'll hit the mission box.

Few salesmen challenge a large husky, seldom an empty bank account, but what man in his right mind would get involved with a poor widow and eight kids?

There is one kind of salesman I simply cannot tolerate. The urchin within me simply cannot resist the temptation to take advantage of my situation when he comes along. He is the long-striding, jaunty, cocky kind who pops in and asks for "the boss." Farmers are plagued by dealers almost as much as housewives. In former days I merely bristled with a "I suppose you mean my husband, sir?" Now I am in position to use every ounce of dramatic ability I can muster and I skillfully employ the script I wanted to use then, but didn't quite dare for fear of Marvin's disapproval.

I greet the unsuspecting culprit with my most innocent, disarming smile: "Why, how do you do?" The salesman replies, "I think you misunderstood, I'd like to see the boss." (One fourth of his self assurance is wiped off.)

"I —"

"Yes, I see. I am the boss, what is it you desire?" (Three fourths of his cockiness wiped away.)

"He — Lady, I meant I wanted to see your *husband!*"

Once I've verified that he isn't the insurance adjuster, the state milk inspector, or some other personage who might be apt to turn the tables on me, I discretely smile and repeat, "Oh that won't be necessary, I do *all* the buying and selling at this house anyway."

Usually at this point the very irritated, angry salesman turns on his heels and dashes off. Only once has this bit of drama continued beyond this last remark. That insistent

117

salesman began screaming, "Your husband, lady, your husband. Can't you see?" to which I replied, "Oh, I'm *so* sorry, I was so sure that I heard you ask for the *boss*." Finally I broke down and ·told him that my husband had died months before.

Admittedly, such an approach is nasty, mean, and unkind, but I just can't resist it. "Boss" indeed!

I do take some commonsensical precautions against careless spending and financial losses which could be brought on by high-pressure salesmanship. When I contemplate the purchase of expensive appliances, trading cars, or buying real-estate, I always seek the help of a man, usually my father or brother-in-law, to do the "dealing." When in doubt concerning a contract, I insist upon having my lawyer study it first. Grief-stricken widows are susceptible to high-pressure salesmen who often work on the emotions. Beginning with the funeral director and monument dealers, one must be constantly on guard. Someone wrote that it would be well if our law makers would make a law invalidating any and all business transactions engaged by a widow for the first six months after her husband's death, unless co-signed by her lawyer. I fully agree.

Also, whenever possible, I trade locally. Occasionally the original purchase price may be a bit more, but valid guarantees of satisfaction as well as competent repair service may prove invaluable to a widow later.

I can't think of a time when someone really took advantage of my widowhood. I hope my friends can say that I have never taken advantage of their kindness and generosity.

CHAPTER SIXTEEN

Who Cares?

*I*T HAPPENED: Disturbed, perplexed, thunder-struck relatives gathered at the quiet, dismal funeral home. Services would begin soon — the final rites for a young father who had taken his life on the very anniversary of his wife's death. Bewildered relatives stared at one another in unbelief and silence. What was there to say? What could anyone say? What message would the pastor bring? except "Why?" Five young orphaned children, stunned into a frightening silence, huddled near one another, unable to fathom the meaning of it all.

The pastor had a message, a painful, startling, shocking one. Following a few soothing words of comfort to the children, he turned abruptly to the relatives and friends. "You question why. You are not guiltless in this death," he remonstrated. "How often this man came to my study, sobbing bitterly, in loneliness. Many times I heard his cry, 'Nobody cares — nobody cares. They don't care.' If each of you gathered here today had given this man, once a month, as much time as you have spent these last two days

119

mourning his death, I don't believe there'd be a funeral to-day."

Those words, "They don't care, no one cares," escaped my lips too — often — during the painfully dark months of severe grief and despondency which followed Marvin's death. I startled and shocked relatives with them, because of my hurt at what seemed their lack of concern. I hurled them again and again as I took note of their obvious pre-occupation with their own families and work, while they seemingly forgot mine. I baffled one good aunt upon meeting her in a parking lot, when she remarked that I was beginning to look so much better. "You appeared so strained and tense the past months," she added.

I retorted, "You knew, you knew; yet you didn't come to help?"

"No one cares. They don't care," are frequent cries of the grieving widow.

Why is it that friends, relatives, community, and church are always ready to give a hand in emergency, quick to render material assistance when it is needed, come forth en masse at the funeral, but seemingly forget the widow's loss and need later, during the period of severe distress when she needs them most?

To be sure, I did have a few of these friends — not everyone forgot. There was the classmate who was always so patient and understanding — so willing and ready to listen to my heartaches and troubles, and another dear friend who made certain that every November 1 (the date of Marvin's death) and June 22nd (our anniversary) would be brightened by a long, cheerful, chatty letter. Dear old aunts, who themselves had experienced the loss of their life partners, wrote often too, with sound advice and dear words of encouragement. A few community people spoke words of reassurance when I met them, and these expressed their faith in my ability to carry on. But it was precisely those friends and relatives (excluding my own family), from whom I expected the most, that I received the least attention. And I cried out, "They don't care!"

Much later, as adjustment took place and after I could reflect a bit more rationally, I realized that in the past I had been guilty of the same behavior. Somehow, after I had once expressed my sympathy to those in mourning at the time of bereavement, I felt satisfied that I had done my part. Certainly my sympathy was heartfelt and sincere at the time that I rendered it. Sometimes I promised myself that I would make a special point of doing something to help later, and then I too would return home, pre-occupied and busy with my family. I didn't mean to be selfish or thoughtless. I simply didn't understand.

Willa Cather, in her book, *O Pioneers,* has Alexandria, the main character, say, "It's by understanding me — that you've helped me. I expect that is the only way one person ever can really help another." Few of those who have not experienced the death of a husband or wife can begin to fathom the total loss. Since Marvin's death I have frequently heard widows exclaim, "One never knows what it is until you experience it yourself."

Onlookers are not aware that grief is often a delayed reaction, and therefore that the time to help the bereaved widow or widower is not during the early period of unfeeling shock, but weeks and even months later when the relentless buildup of day upon day of loneliness begins to gnaw and strangle and suffocate his or her entire being. If only others could grasp the meaning of a widower's words, as I perceived them, when he cried six months after the death of his wife, "They [friends and relatives] say I'm getting along all right. I am — IN A WAY. Sure, we eat and work. I hire someone to clean and wash. I've picked up my business again. But, oh, if they could only know this," he continued, as he pressed his fist to his breast. Tears fell as he repeated, "If they could only know this."

And if they did understand, if they did know? Many times when I point out the need of others, I am greeted with the argumentative lament, "But how can I help? I never know what to do or say." Why has consolation become a lost art among mankind? Possibly because we feel some large, magnanimous gesture is necessary, when the little things so easily performed are overlooked. A cheery note, an invitation out, a visit, or even a phone call can bring pleasure and comfort to the lonely one.

Lack of knowledge concerning the widow's plight is accompanied by failure to understand the widow herself. Although our society offers no cut-and-dried ritual or a set of rules, somehow it does expect the widow to be different — and she is! The traumatic shock and severe disturbances she has experienced can not help but affect her personality. As a result, former friends are often uncomfortable with her. Suddenly she becomes incongruous within the very circle of which she was once a part.

I remember too vividly the awkward pauses and moments of silence as I approached groups of former friends. On one occasion, when I was invited to a small house party consisting of all married couples with whom my husband and I had previously associated, the conversation turned to anniversary dates and years. I saw the hostess bite her lip — obviously sorry about the course of discussion and my silence. I could "feel" her pondering as to whether she would have been more kind to have left me out than to have invited me to join a group in which I would be so vividly reminded that I was alone.

I bit my lip too, not because I couldn't discuss recent anniversaries, but because once more I sensed the uncomfortable, widening gap between the others and myself, when I wanted so desperately to remain a part of them. The processes of segregation and exclusion from the normal "man-woman" world, especially for the younger widow, is as inevitable as if she were condemned to a penitentiary for women. Yet she remains a parent and a woman.

It is not completely surprising, though, that society is uncomfortable with the widow — she is ill at ease with herself too. She too senses and feels that she is different. For fifteen years I had thought of myself as Marvin's wife, identifying and measuring the id through his eyes. Suddenly I was a lost soul. Before marriage I had been a distinct individual on my own — but I didn't know myself after Marvin died. I knew even less about what was expected of me, but I was aware that a change was expected. The customary, casual relationships with my friends and their husbands suddenly became quite different without a husband in the background. Former behavior could be easily misconstrued by husbands and more surely by their wives. I needed laughter; I wanted to weep; yet I wasn't sure that society would approve of either.

I wasn't aware either that the full impact of loss would be delayed. Perhaps if I had known, I would have taken more care to express my need for visits and help right from the beginning, rather than foolishly giving the impression that I was getting along all right, in order to ward off pity. If I had known ahead of time how desperately I would need help later, I would have replaced that guest book in the funeral home with a calendar, asking each visitor to designate a day in the *future* on which he would console by way of a visit, a card, or a call! A bit unorthodox perhaps, but at least later I wouldn't have found the hundreds of tokens of sympathy afforded me those first few hours as useless as twenty ice cream cones handed to a starving child on a warm summer day, who is then left all but forgotten by her benefactors.

If only someone could have told me that this grief was a necessary step toward adjustment, that a day would come when the heavy ache would subside and life become meaningful again. Unfortunately, there are no courses to be taken in preparation for widowhood — and if there were, who would take them? Widowhood only descends on the *other* woman.

Although I felt very keenly about what I designated at the time as neglect on the part of relatives and friends, it was the lack of consideration on the part of my church which pained me most, perhaps because I had always thought of the church as the chief instrument of compassion and love, of bearing and sharing one another's burdens. Yet my church was not there to help. For a whole year after the funeral not a single representative had called. Only one family had paid mine a visit, once an invitation was extended. All the "ice cream cones" were handed out in the first few hours of grief. Of course, on Sundays I heard the pastor and congregation pray for God's blessing upon the widow, but why, I wondered, was the congregation so reluctant to help God along a little: It's like praying for missionaries to bring the gospel to the heathen and then adding, "but don't ask us to do it." How often the church forgets that she is the very instrument which God has ordained to carry out His work. In spite of the fact that the form for the ordination of officers in my church specifies that part of their duty is to be the "relief of the distressed, both with kindly deeds and words of consolation and cheer from Scripture," such visits were not forthcoming.

It would be unfair to single out my church. Since my loss I have corresponded frequently with other widows and widowers. Almost invariably their experiences coincide with mine. One young widow wrote, "My church visited me once in the seven years I've been left alone." Another stated that she had been visited twice in five years. One lady from the West wrote, "My husband was the pastor's right hand. He served as the vice president of the church council, yet in the two and one-half years since his death neither the pastor nor any council member has visited me and my five children. All I ever received was a pat on the shoulder one morning after church, with a 'You're doing fine' from the pastor. How did he know?"

Nor have I found the church active in consolation or "burden lifting" in other distressing emotional disturbances. One mother, turned prematurely gray by the scandalous life of her only wayward son, lamented, "The church is no help. It comes often to deal out disciplinary measures to my son, yet no church officer or member ever came to console my grieving heart."

In my hurt and despair it was natural to judge, "My church doesn't care." Yet, I am the church too. To condemn her is to condemn myself as well. Why does there

125

seem to be such a lack of concern for one another within Christ's fold?

Is it the age? Materialism? Everyone seems so pre-occupied with his own financial success, maintaining status comparable to that of his neighbor, climbing the social ladder, that there is no time left for the deeper and more abiding things of life, much less for bearing one another's burdens.

Perhaps it is lack of understanding here too. Not a single member of my church council has experienced the loss of a life partner. How could they know the severe problems and pain involved in the process of readjustment? And if they know, how will they help? Big business and industry train personnel people and public relations experts. There is no such training ground in my church, no courses in guidance, counseling, or the understanding of psychological forces. These men have the greatest message of comfort, yet they are left untrained in presenting it.

I do recognize that church officers are busy people. This was particularly true during the time following the death of my husband. My church was without a pastor, and extra burdens fell upon the already overloaded church officers. It was their business to maintain the church, preserve doctrine, provide and manage budgets, keep the pulpit supplied and the building in repair, as well as tend to discipline problems, the aged, the needy, and the emotionally disturbed. Many of these same men are chosen as leaders in their schools and communities as well. Besides all this, they are expected to maintain their own businesses and provide for their families. Small wonder they can barely find time to visit the widows.

Yet, within the camp of the church lies a large force

of help, virtually untapped for generations — her women. Could it be that my church, in its attempt to carry out the Pauline instructions pertaining to office bearers, has leaned over backwards and lost sight of the feminine qualities of understanding, mercy, and soul healing? Is it forgetting that although Eve was created to be a helpmeet for Adam, that she also was his partner in dressing the garden? Ironically, it was a Martha who added much to Christ's physical comfort and a Mary who washed his feet and soothed his soul with an alabaster jar of ointment. Yet, womanhood has atrophied in the pew for so long that now it can hardly do more than move from one bench to another; meanwhile, the art of extending deep feeling, mercy, and consolation is becoming nearly extinct.

Within the shadow of my church lies a hospital, where patients remain week after week, with never a visit. A few blocks farther down the street is a rest home for the aged, where old, bed-ridden patients cry, "Don't forget us, don't forget." Within my church are scores of women so bored with life that they must find part-time employment to keep them occupied. Organizing deaconesses under the direction of the deacons or elders might be a solution. After generations of passive women, doing such would be a big challenge to any church council. It would take scheduling and supervision, reports and conferences, pleadings and reassurances, assignments and education; yet what a force we women could become visiting the sick, welcoming the stranger, seeking out the distressed, consoling the mournful, not only within the congregation but in the entire community, doing these in the name of our Savior.

Perhaps as each wife involved her husband, and the children imitated their mother, the lost art of consolation, the concern for each other, and the bearing of one another's burdens might return and burn brightly in succeeding generations.

The story of the widower? It happened. I have seen the two headstones which testify to its veracity. It didn't happen in *my* church — yet.

CHAPTER SEVENTEEN

Lonely and Alone

*D*URING THE MANY LONG MONTHS when I had known that my loved one would all too soon be leaving my side, I had somewhat prepared myself for the utter loneliness I would know at his departure. I was aware (of course, only in part) that I would miss our long evening talks, our mutual interest in the lives of our eight children, the sharing of the joys and sorrows and problems. I knew, too (though not fully then), that I would indeed miss his glance of love, the clasp of his hand, his warm embrace at the day's end, and our silent conversations when just being together made everything seem all right. I was prepared to some little extent for this loss, but little had I realized that my husband's death would mean losing not only him and all that he meant to me, but also my whole social world. It had never occurred to me that current friends, the families we visited and those who visited us, the couples we dined with, the crowd we chummed with — that all of this too would be wiped away.

And I was hurt, angry, and resentful. Why, I thought,

the early Egyptian custom of burying the family with the deceased husband was kinder than this. Hadn't I suffered enough in the loss of my husband, without suffering the loss of my whole world? Time after time I had asked old friends to come after church, or to spend an evening with us, but the best I managed was a few lady friends for afternoon tea. Men just don't visit where there is no man, and hostesses can't be bothered with setting an odd number at the table. And so I was literally hurled into an all-children and, at best, feminine world.

My reactions to the pressing need for adult companionship were no compliment to me. I reacted first of all with a hurt bewilderment, then anger and resentment. "It's unfair; it's simply not right. It's not even Christian," were thoughts that repeated themselves over and over; and how I wanted to shout them from the very housetop and even to hurt as I had been hurt. As time went along, I reversed my behavior, weeping, feeling sorry for myself, and gradually drawing myself apart from even the few offers of friendship I did receive.

Once in a psychology class a professor had drawn on the chalkboard a picture of a high wall and had labeled it *Frustration*. "Students," he said, "there are only three ways one can meet this wall." First he drew an arrow directly into the wall. This, he implied, was the reaction of anger, aggressiveness, of continually bumping one's head against a situation, hurting only oneself. Then he drew a second arrow, away from the wall. This represented the person who was reacting just as immaturely as the first, pulling himself into a corner, withdrawing, feeling sorry for himself. Frequently these are the mentally depressed cases we so often hear of. The third arrow the instructor drew neatly around the wall. This reaction, he assured us, was really the only mature one.

In my hurt and resentment I had done a good job of using the first two of these reactions and had managed to solve nothing. It was precisely at this point — when I first sat down with myself and realized that if I was to end this wall of frustration I would have to make constructive attempts to get around it — that things began to look up. "Lord," I prayed, "You know my need for friends, both male and female, my need for a social world. I've reacted foolishly; now take over and help me to see things I might do to fill this need."

The first thing that presented itself had been there all the time; it was the opportunity to take in some evening college courses. I had always enjoyed learning and studying, and I felt this would provide an excellent outside interest. It did indeed, but it proved far more valuable in the fact that for three wonderful hours each week I could drop the role of mother and widow and become a woman. I realize that not everyone would enjoy such a diversion, but for those with other tastes every community has its civic committees, gym classes at the Y, bowling teams, and other activities. There is always the chance of a stimulating outside part-time job. Two qualifications should be met in finding such an escape: one, the new interest should be stimulating, and two, if at all possible it should provide a normal relationship with both men and women. I think, too, that any widow, although it will be painful at first, should take advantage of any mixed groups and gatherings in her community.

Once when I was bitter at being left out, a friend had said, "It's a shame our community does not have an organization for those left alone." I had retorted quite angrily, "Thanks for pointing out so graciously where I belong." But now as I realized that society was not likely to change for me, perhaps I had better begin concentrating on finding friends among single persons. The first attempts were not completely satisfying, not because it is impossible to find real companionship among other widows, or single persons, but because the friendship I sought was not likely to be built on something as meager as a common loss — any more than a hasty remarriage contracted only to reduce loneliness is likely to be a strong and good one. I surely am not against remarriage; but as for myself, I would be prone to prove to myself first that I am mature enough to make a satisfying life alone. I would not like to reduce marriage to being simply a crutch on which to lean my own weakness.

But there are other ways to attract friends. One I have found is as simple as inviting two families to my home at once, letting each know that I've invited the other. This of course takes planning, as I once discovered when I'd almost invited two congenial families without first counting noses. As one of my children said when I discussed the invitation, "Great, Mom, that should be a ball with, let's see, twenty, no, twenty-one kids all at once." Needless to say I did a little switching. But we did have company that Sunday night for coffee.

CHAPTER EIGHTEEN

Not for Fixing Faucets

PING, PING, PING. The leaky faucet was unrelenting in its message of needing repair. For three nights I had vowed that tomorrow something would be done about it, yet each day I had managed to procrastinate. The continuous splashing of the water drops against the porcelain sink was persistent and annoying, keeping me from sleep.

"No better time than right now," I decided as I stumbled out of bed. Gingerly I crossed the cold porch in my bare feet to where the tools were kept in a cabinet.

I gathered every tool in sight: pliers, wrenches, hammer, screw drivers, and just to make sure, Marv's two large pipe wrenches.

With the pliers firmly gripping the faucet, I twisted and turned, only to discover that it didn't unscrew as easily for me as it had for my husband. The innocent-looking pipe wrench seemed made-to-order. For the first time in my life I really grasped the principal of the lever — after one good, healthy tug the faucet flew out of my hand and was followed by a surge of water gushing straight at me. Too late I remembered Marvin's instructions: "Now there is one faucet that doesn't shut off with this valve; that one is on a direct line from the well, and you can only shut it off here next to the pump."

"This had to be *that* one faucet," I lamented as I slid over the wet, slippery kitchen floor and down the icy-cold basement stairs.

If there was one area in which Marvin must have felt concern about my ability to carry on without him, it would have been in the line of the mechanical. How impatient he had been at times at my complete incompetence with tools. Over and over he had laughed at my "woman's" grasp of the hammer (in the middle or near the head instead of at the end). How irritated he had become when he asked for a wood screw and I brought him a metal screw, or a bolt instead of a nut. Once, when he was attempting to teach me how to drive a car and I kept forgetting to push in the clutch, he asked me if I had the slightest idea of what a gear was. When I shook my head dubiously, he shouted, "Didn't you even have physics in high school?"

He could only shake his head in amazement when I assured him that I had had such a course and passed it too! I didn't bother to tell him that the very same teacher had once cautioned me after an aptitude test, "You seem to have natural ability in the persuasive fields, writing, teaching, and selling, but don't ever try to make a living doing mechanical work!"

Because of this lack on my part, I suppose it is not surprising that in our last years together Marvin alluded to his oncoming death by simple little warnings such as, "Never try to fix anything electrical until the main switch has been pulled," or "Be sure to remember that the furnace needs new filters once in awhile." When a few weeks before his death he reminded me that the red can of oil was the right one for the car when the weather turned cold, my heart screamed, "Do you mean you won't be here then?" but I merely nodded my head and turned aside quickly. I discovered after he was gone that many of the very same instructions had been repeated to the older children, displaying even further evidence of his lack of faith in my ability to cope with the mechanical and the technical.

Not only did he give verbal instructions. When ever any small appliance needed fixing, he insisted that I sit beside him, "to help," he added. Together we fixed plug ends, cleaned pulsators for milking machines, oiled parts of the pump, changed oil in the lawn mower, and fixed faucets. Painstakingly he taught me the shut-off valves to the water lines, the ones to the barn, to the softener, and the ones to the hoghouse. I learned how and where to disconnect the water pump, the gas valves to the water heater, the gas valves to milk-house appliances, and above all, the various electrical switches.

It's a terrible thing to watch a man die by inches — I should not like to live through it again — but I shudder to think how ill-prepared I would have been had we not had the warning and much time to prepare for his death.

How proudly I could display the many skills I've acquired since he left — if he could come back. How I would like to tell him about the leaky chicken waterers and how I repaired them by replacing those tiny T-shaped washers. I would show him the new belt on the water pump, the many plug ends I've repaired, all the house screens with brand new screening stretched and tacked in place.

I'd tell him of the night that the water softener kept running, and how by wiggling just the right mechanism I got it stopped. He'd have to hear about the neat trick I learned to control leaky water cups in the cattle barn, too. I can almost hear him say, "I knew you could!"

Would he laugh when I told him that the one single mechanical device which requires the indispensable services of a husband is the long zipper in the middle back of all my best dresses. Wouldn't he chuckle as I demonstrated how I've tried tying strings to the pull, yet still managed to snag the dress material right in the middle where the waist line is a little snug.

Or would he in utter frustration react as he did occasionally when he was condemned to his chair, "I might just as well be dead, I'm no help to you anyhow."

I answered at those times by reminding him that we needed *him* — not just the work of his hands. How much more adequately I can express it now: "No, my darling, it isn't your work, your salary, nor even the fixing of faucets and switches that we need you for. We need *you,* your love and pride in us. I need your sense of humor when silly little affairs upset me. I need your voice at night when I come home to a quiet house. When wonderful, lovely things happen, or the children make cute remarks which have to be shared, you are not there to tell. I even need you to tell me off at times when my silly feminine whims and fancies get out of hand, and oh, how I need to be needed! I need *you* in a thousand ways, not the things you do — just *you.*" If only he could. . . .

And then I remember how often I must have measured and rated myself by the things I did. How often I brought him my offerings when he needed *me,* my concern, my love, or a word of encouragement perhaps.

It is so easy to become indispensable in our own eyes when we begin to count the things we do, and forget that our great gift is ourself, our heart.

At times, I'm sure, I come to God like that, too, bearing little works, withholding my heart, bringing the gifts and not the giver.

CHAPTER NINETEEN

My Cows Are Not For Sale

I STILL CHUCKLE WHEN I REMEMBER HIM — that funny little cattle-buyer, retreating backwards toward the barn door, his hands guarding his face as if to shield himself from the verbal attack which I had launched in his direction.

It was hot — steamy, sweltering, humidity-high hot! Moreover, it had been hot like that for nine days without relief. I was late at the barn — that was caused by the heat too. The Sunday night before had been a sleepless one due to the heat, and I had overslept in the early morning coolness.

Perhaps because it was Monday, or perhaps because of the heat, I had a serious case of "feeling-sorry-for-yourself-itis." I was remembering the berries to be picked, the baskets of laundry just sitting there like squatting ducks waiting for me, the potatoes to be hoed with children who wanted to go fishing instead, and the cows which were pokier than ever. This morning I hated it all, and my cows were on the receiving end of my vengeance.

138

Cows! What other animals would demand attention at the two worst hours of the day, early in the morning when I'd rather be in bed, or the late hours when all my energy had already been drained away by cleaning, mopping, washing, baking, and settling insignificant quarrels among the children? What other manufacturing agency would require the constant shoveling in of raw materials from before and the constant shoveling out of an *equal* amount of waste material from behind, and still produce a product? For that matter, what other animals could stare at you with those moony, vacant eyes, yet sense an open gate forty acres away? It was not that I couldn't appreciate the value and appearance of fine milk cows; the four of mine were among the finest in the country. But on that hot, sweltering morning I just couldn't warm up to them! Their demanding schedule seemed to be a curse instead of a blessing.

Hot tears stung my eyes, and my aching heart murmured again, "Why? Why could even then other farmers' wives be busy preparing nourishing breakfasts for their husbands, wives who were dressed in pretty frocks in cool kitchens while I had to be there in that hot-box in dungarees, struggling with bossy to relinquish her product, I who loved my kitchen, I who was never happier than when I could turn out delicious meals for the one I loved so dearly?" Angrily I slammed the bucket of foaming milk against the milk can, managing to spill much of it over my legs and feet.

Now if I hadn't had such a serious case of feeling sorry for myself I might have heard a small voice reminding me that not many widows had a lovely farm with a spacious farmyard and an ample house shaded all day long by delightfully-large maple trees. I might have heard the voice reminding me of the large pitchers of rich milk my little ones took for granted, the extra groceries I could purchase from the biweekly milk checks, all of which those bossies were responsible for. It was the garden, the farm, the cows, and the chickens which made it possible to care for my eight lovely children and yet be able to remain at home.

Of course the serious malady of self-pity doesn't only affect the hearing; it mars the vision too, or I might have been visualizing Monday night's supper — large bowls of fresh strawberries, topped with sugar and swimming in rich dairy cream, accompanied by huge slabs of homemade bread still warm enough to melt our own homemade butter. Why, if it hadn't been for that little man who appeared on the scene just then, who knows, I might be all the way crippled by now.

He entered the barn just after I had spilled all that lovely milk. Erroneously he had heard that I was considering selling my cows, and I was quite aware that he intended to buy them for his price, making sure that he would reap a "little profit" in reselling them. Yet on that hot morning, ridding myself of the animals was certainly tempting. I felt quite certain that although I maintained that I did not plan to sell at that time, he sensed my mood of the morning as he paced from one cow to the other, punching one here, another there, finding a little flaw in each. Then he approached me with his price, despite my insistence that I did not intend to sell. Standing there, with his two thumbs stretching out elastic suspenders which were hardly able to hold up his baggy pants, he spoke the mortal words, "Lady, why you work so hard? Move to city; you easy get fifty dolla's a kid from welfare, and you do nothing."

I can't even remember the rest of the episode, at least not the violent outburst which caused him to retreat, repeating over and over, "I sorry lady, no offense."

Sell my cows indeed! — I, who even then used our bank's service window to cash my Social Security checks, to which I had real claim, because I felt guilty for receiving them nevertheless — I who wanted so badly to teach my sons responsibility and respect for honest work so they could become men like their dad.

Many times in our married life my husband had accused me of arrogant self-dependence, and rightfully so. Independence is not always the greatest of virtues, especially in a marriage relationship, but then, neither is indolence and immature dependence.

Even now I find it difficult to accept gestures of help gracefully. It is a kindness to let others help and I try very hard to remind myself of that, but to accept public hand-outs while physical strength and mental ability allow me to make my own way, I could never do.

Even though I strongly resented the cattle buyer's suggestion to sit back and live on county aid, I would have applied for public benefits rather than leave my small pre-school child to the care of a baby-sitter for several hours a day while I worked. Children suffering from the shock of losing one parent deserve at least the presence and care of the other. Attempting to do the normal work of two people, with the accompanying fatigue and frustration, would find me less than a mother, even in the hours which I could spend with them.

Welfare agencies are wonderful institutions when used to help those who are in real need of them — disabled fathers and mothers, widows of very small children who

142

can not care for their children and work too, those living in poverty areas where the community can not provide sufficient working opportunities — but handouts have a way of eating away our self-pride, self-respect, and independence. The price is high — too high for me.

However, the Department of Welfare does offer services which go beyond the financial handouts, and a wise widow will take advantage of them. I am truly sorry that I did not take advantage of their family guidance and counseling clinic. Somehow, I had been always under the impression that these offices were only concerned with therapy for unstable, disturbed marriages, broken homes, and foster children. I did not realize that they are happy to advise perplexed and bewildered widows too. This department also has the latest information on various forms of federal aid for the single parent, such as educational grants for both herself and her children, and also benefits through anti-poverty programs. In some instances even her baby-sitting fees are provided by the government while the widow finishes her education. This organization also gladly furnishes referrals to psychological and medical agencies who can provide assistance.

While it is true that the undeserving often take advantage of the Welfare Department, yet there is nothing degrading about using these facilities when actual need exists. Indeed, this is precisely the reason for which they have been established.

"No sir, my cows aren't for sale yet, not until I'm able to care for my family without sacrificing my children's well-being."

CHAPTER TWENTY

Either Rich or Poor

OUR SOCIETY REALLY KNOWS only two types of widows: The rich, young, glamorous, enticing type is the kind which unattached men had better beware of. One meets her often in soap operas and poor literature. The other is the poor widow, invariably dressed in drab, worn clothes; her face is drawn and haggard from life's struggle to make ends meet. Her expression is either one of suffering or grim bitterness. Her children are neat and clean, but just one step above the rags of poverty.

Ironically, the line between the two is not a hard and fast one. It is quite possible to belong to both categories at the same time, depending upon the observer and the observed behavior. One widow of only a few months expressed it so adequately when she observed, "I'm either in the poor house or on a rich man's farm." Everyone has heard of them: The widow who struggles and pinches pennies to give her children a week at camp or a college education — "Where does she get her money?" The widow who dares to buy a new car — "She must have a stack somewhere!"

Few young widows are financially flush, yet this is not necessarily an evil. The need to provide for her family may well be the first call beckoning her back to life. Preoccupation with this concern often directs her mind away from her loss and rescues her from the clutches of self-pity.

How fortunate I was to have these financial matters settled before Marvin's death. The attorney's help proved as invaluable after Marvin's death as before. A good lawyer is one friend no widow should be without. Many of his practical suggestions helped me at a time when deep shock made clear thinking difficult. When I received the insurance monies, it was my attorney who suggested that I use part of it for family household necessities, rather than to pay all of it down upon the farm mortgage. "You will probably never have any sizeable amounts of cash available again," he recommended. "Get the new furnace, a better car, and appliances which may need replacing soon, now, rather than pay heavy interest or carrying charges on these items later." I did just that. Huge orders of blankets, bedding, and dishes went out — Marvin's long illness and resulting medical bills made it impossible to replace these earlier. I converted the old coal furnace to a convenient oil one. A new electric range and a good used refrigerator soon replaced the ones I had been using for over fifteen years.

He was right — there never has been a large cash account since. He also advised me to withhold even more of the insurance money and place it into negotiable bonds. "Emergencies frequently arrive," he explained, "and it is advisable to have some money available to avoid taking out mortgages against your property." Once more he proved trustworthy in his judgment. Before one year had elapsed after Marvin's death, I was confronted with the need of drilling a new 150-foot well, since the old one had become contaminated. This required a brand new submersible water pump. A few months later an underground leak necessitated a new water line to the barn. Then electrical shorts developed in the barn wiring and it needed replacement. Old Tizzie, the family car, broke down, another big expenditure. My only regret was that I hadn't followed my lawyer's suggestion of doubling the amount that I did place into bonds.

It was my trusted attorney, too, who acquainted us with several avenues of assistance, both county and state: interest-free loans and other helps toward temporary relief from mounting hospital and medical bills. He also made arrangements with the local Social Security office for the application for disability benefits during Marvin's illness and later for widow's pension and death payments. Even today, he stands ready to examine the small print on contracts about which I may be dubious. He is always willing to give counsel concerning financial problems.

To lighten her burden, modern society has provided several sources of aid, although quite unfairly in proportion to what it is doing for the widower. First of all, if she is a mother of young children, she will likely be covered by a widow's pension program under the Federal Social Security Act and/or some private pension program. While the Social Security plan may not prove adequate in itself, especially if a widow has more than three children, since the maximum payment is reached with that number, it can certainly go a long way toward meeting her family's needs.

146

Chances are that her husband, in the present day at least, may have served with the armed services. If so, she is entitled to a veteran's pension as well. Most likely her husband also carried G.I. life insurance. It is extremely important for her, therefore, to contact both her local Social Security office and the Veteran's Administration immediately. Two vitally important records she must provide are her husband's Social Security number and his discharge papers.

Frequently financial decisions are made too hastily and under a severe strain, when clear thinking and careful planning are almost impossible. Well-meaning friends, often with diverse advice, frequently tend only to confuse and complicate matters. Most widows would do well to postpone any major changes and moves as long as possible, living one day at a time, making decisions of only the most immediate urgency. Radical changes should be made only in extreme emergencies, especially where young children are involved. Moving to another area, or even to another house may be as traumatic for the child as the father's death. One emotional upheaval is enough, without the additional burden of a second. It may be that as time goes on the widow will find her home too large, lavish, or expensive, and it is simply practical to buy a smaller one, but usually such a move can be postponed for a few months at least. Often such moves in the early days of grief are more an escape mechanism than actual need. The familiar rooms, furniture, and home where two had once lived in love and harmony become painful reminders after one partner dies, but another home or city will not bring the loved one back. It may in fact even delay positive readjustment.

Whether rich or poor, or somewhere between the two

extremes, a widow will face all kinds of economic and financial problems which call for solution. With good legal counsel, a good dose of common sense, and prayer for God's guidance, these problems may be resolved before they develop into traumatic experiences.

CHAPTER TWENTY ONE

The Third Choice

*M*OST HOUSEWIVES SEEM TO THINK that there are only two choices regarding family finances: staying at home or taking a job. There is really a third choice: staying at home *and* working. Budget-stretching can become a full-time job for any homemaker. It may help to spread a husband's income as much as adding a second check.

Fortunately, we live on a farm which itself provides endless opportunities for stretching pennies. There is our annual garden. Beginning with rhubarb, asparagus, and then followed in June by quarts and quarts of strawberries, I was launched full-swing into the freezing and canning season. July brought string beans (usually one hundred quarts, picked, snipped, and frozen or canned), peas, and pickles, followed by bushels of tomatoes (winter's vitamin C) and cabbages grated into a ten-gallon jar of kraut.

Picking up potatoes was always a family event: the more eaters, the more pickers; even my little toddler helped by filling his syrup bucket. Soon forty to fifty bushels of them in the bin would be joined by huge piles of squash and pumpkins.

Our apple orchard was the source for gallons of apple sauce, row upon row of pickled crabs, a whole shelf of apple slices destined for future pies and desserts, and jar upon jar of tempting jellies and apple butter.

Cold, snappy weather ended the garden season, but not the canning; for then our attention would turn to the fat, lazy hens which had to be culled from their more productive cohorts. If such hens were not available from our own flock, we purchased one hundred to one hundred-fifty. Of course, we missed Dad, who had always extended a willing hand. He was extremely fond of chicken, and he could not resist putting away many of them for a hungry family. He skillfully hung each chicken by one leg from my clothesline, usually a dozen at a time, then performed the nasty job of beheading them. He had always emphasized that bleeding chickens properly was an important step in the butchering process, and he trusted no one else with this procedure.

Everyone pitched in to undress the chickens. Feathers literally flew in all directions as the chore was accomplished. The "inside job" was left for Mom. Usually one-half of the hens were packaged and placed into the freezer for future roasting and frying. Their canned sisters would later find themselves swimming in rich pot-pie gravy, diced into salads, or mixed into tempting hot dishes. Steaming bowls of chicken-rice soup were especially welcome on cold winter days.

Not all our food savings were the direct result of rural living, however. Soaps, fruits, sugar, cereals, and syrup were always purchased in the largest size available. Syrup by the gallon costs nearly fifty per cent less than when purchased in four separate quarts. I purchase raisins, brown sugar, confectioners sugar at wholesale stores in ten-pound lots, at a savings of five cents a pound or more. A hundred pounds of flour is quickly turned into baked good needs when one has eight hungry children to satisfy. The fact that we couldn't afford shopping at our local bakery was quite unimportant since Mom could bake delicious bread, rolls, donuts, pies, cakes, and cookies at home, at a fraction of the purchase price at the bakery. Few forms of creativity gave me more satisfaction than producing baked goods from scratch with flour and a few cupboard staples. Seeing a row of steaming brown loaves of bread, cooling buns, or frosted sweet rolls still hot and fresh from the oven always fills me with a sense of accomplishment which would be hard to match in a full-time job.

Stretching the budget wasn't limited to food savings. The first really serious argument between Marvin and myself had been over the purchase of a sewing machine. Since I had never sewn a stitch before marriage, I couldn't see wasting all that money on an expensive sewing machine. You'll learn," was Marvin's only comment — and as usual he was right.

Fortunately, necessity is the mother of attempt as well as invention. Before long I was not only making my clothes, and that of the children, but remaking them. Ladies' coats were turned inside out, recut, and patterned into little girls' coats; sun suits originated from used skirts and dresses, tiny slips from the backs of men's shirts. Kitchen curtains and living room drapes were also born under the needle of my machine. When I realized that there was no money with which to replace Marvin's favorite platform rocker, I slit the upholstery straight down the middle, using one half for a pattern, keeping the other intact to guide me in putting the odd-shaped pieces back together. A glow of pride filled me as my efforts took on a professional appearance. Since then I have also recovered our davenport, all with the same sewing machine — indeed Marvin was right when he insisted, "You'll learn," and it has been a satisfying education.

I have also learned to do my own painting. Inevitably, every time we moved, we found a pink kitchen. Anyone who knows me well knows my very silly but strong aversion to pink in any form. Landlords aren't likely to bow to something as absurd as color aversion, but I was most unhappy in such a situation. While Marvin could not share my intolerance of the color, he was sympathetic and made it sound so simple by offering me money for paint of a color which suited me. Painting was one area, however, in which he flatly refused his assistance. My first attempts were frustrating. Improper handling of the brush and roller brought down more splashes on my kitchen floor than on the ceiling. Once Marvin did ask casually if I was painting the wall or myself, but practice made for perfection. Soon I found other rooms in the house looking drab in comparison to my sunny yellow kitchen. Before long the entire house was redecorated, fresh, and pretty.

With the birth of a third son, Marvin had decided it was time to purchase a home barbering set, and he also determined that it was I who would learn the new trade, so he could get home haircuts too. Emily did little to reassure me on my first attempt when she reminded me that Dad couldn't keep his hat on in church next Sunday to cover up my experiment. Today that twelve-dollar clipper set has produced over one thousand hair cuts. By watching my hair dresser taper my little daughter's hair once, I learned to do the trimming, styling, and tapering for all four daughters as well.

Stretching the budget wasn't something that had to be put into practice when I became a widow; it simply became a matter of course at our house way back in the early years of our marriage. Neither Marvin nor I approved of a mother working outside of the home. Marvin worked very hard, even taking in night work at times to supplement our meager income from dairying. Later he coupled a summer construction job with farming, but he made it plain that it was up to me to manage on these earnings. That meant work and ingenuity.

That third choice, staying at home and working, means just that, but it can mean deep satisfaction in one's own creativity, as well as a challenge to ingenuity. Budget stretching at home does not involve expenses associated with an outside job, such as baby-sitter's fees, car costs, and clothes, besides the wear and tear, the hurry and fatigue, the time clock and rush hour stress. I'm very glad I learned the art of budget stretching while it was chiefly a labor of love. Marvin's deep appreciation for my efforts not only made the hard work rewarding, but bound us into a close-knit partnership. I found it difficult to carry on these activities during the first few months after his death. My little toddler asked if I forgot how to bake "them yummy buns," and the older children frowned at my shabby housekeeping or my personal appearance. Through such remarks I once again became aware of the satisfaction in serving these eight beautiful lives by making the most with little, thereby creating an atmosphere of beauty and well-being.

Part Four

Life Calls Again

CHAPTER TWENTY TWO

Things Are Looking Up

*N*O, I WON'T SPEND ANOTHER DAY like I did last year," I firmly told myself.

Decisively I snatched the cord from the wall socket, set the iron down, then tossed the basket of dampened clothes into the corner. Quickly I threw open the kitchen window and called to the boys out on the lawn, "Get out the tackle and poles; we're going fishing."

All week long I had been steeling myself against this day — the 22nd of June — our wedding anniversary date. This would have been our seventeenth together; now it was my second alone. I tried to ignore the calendar, but the black numerals continued to glare at me from the kitchen wall. Again and again I told myself that this year could not be a repetition of last June 22.

"Nature is doing her best," I observed, as I had awakened to one of those perfect June days, brilliant and beautiful. The air was filled with the fragrance of freshly-cut hay; there was not a cloud overhead. It was cool enough to need a sweater, but the air held a promise of penetrating warmth just around the corner. The milking had gone smoothly enough too. Breakfast brought just a little sob as my eye caught the black 22 at the top of our daily meditation booklet. I managed to stifle it — no one remembered "my day."

Shortly after the breakfast dishes had been neatly stacked away the gas delivery man came. My hands shook as I penned "June 22" on the check I wrote him. Determined to win with mind over heart, I hauled out the weekly ironing. That was a bad choice. The quiet task was not conducive to forgetting, and it wasn't long before one tear and then another dropped with a hissing sound onto my hot iron.

"I didn't have to iron, did I?" Nature was too beautiful to waste anyway. "Get out, that might help," I told myself. "Do something nice."

What nicer thing can a mother do than take her boys fishing? The boys had made a subtle hint yesterday that a fishing trip was long overdue. These impatient lads decided to do a bit of practicing while I was gone picking strawberries. It seems that David managed to catch the telephone wires on his first cast. By the time I arrived home they had retrieved it and the whole line, all tangled neatly in one little ball, was waiting for an unsuspecting mother. At least one line was in readiness. Hadn't I spent all last night unraveling it?

It didn't take the boys very long to tie the poles to the right side of the car, and to place the worms, tackle, and rods in the truck — no longer than it took me to toss a few quarts of milk, a loaf of bread, some cans of luncheon meat and tuna, mayonnaise, and fruit into our ever-ready picnic basket.

The children scrambled into the car, then scrambled out again. Of course. The poles were tied to the right side of the car, and those who were supposed to sit on that side were still out, while the ones who had chosen the left windows to sit next to, were already in — in the way for the others to get where they wanted to be. It just seemed easier to pile out and start over again. My hand reached out to turn the switch, then stopped as I remembered our last fishing trip, the time we arrived at the lake without the bait. (The time before that our picnic lunch had been left behind on the kitchen table.) Just to make sure, I climbed out for a last-minute checkup. I checked too closely! What could that terrible odor be?

"O.K. boys, start explaining this mess," I shouted as I pulled the worm bucket from the trunk.

It turned out that some guilty boy (of course, not one of them) had kept the worms well watered, swimming, in fact.

"Toss it out; drowned worms won't interest live fish," I screamed. It took several moments of deliberation to decide that the best place to dump them was behind the garden, some distance away — the best time was right then!

"At least it's better to know when we start out that we don't have worms, than to get to the lake without them like last time, isn't it Mom?" one of them dared to venture.

"Oh, yes, much better!"

And this had started out as something 'nice' to do! Once again we scrambled into the car. This time only two of the children got in the wrong order, and they managed to wiggle past the seated ones. We were off at last.

With four little boys needing worms on their hooks, taking fish off the hooks, retrieving hooks from snagged sweatshirts, and untangling lines, there wasn't much time for remembering "the day". I suppose the fish knew we were there; they were given enough opportunity to hear us. At any rate they must have decided to wait a bit before seeking breakfast — or maybe it was their rest between breakfast and lunch. Fishing just wasn't good. Jerry, the youngest, was the first to tire of it. "Fishin's *work,*" he exclaimed, "at least it's not *playin'!*" With that he dropped his pole and ran off to the adjoining playground for a spin on the merry-go-round. Ever-impatient David followed close at his heels. Before long, four deserted poles were lying along the water's edge, all fishing forgotten. It wasn't that we hadn't caught anything. Beside three small fish, we had chalked up one tennis shoe (unhooked), a mound of algae (unhooked), two sweatshirts (still hooked — just the boys out), and one very tall elm tree (still hooked). It was just that this wasn't exciting enough for the explosive energy of four charged batteries.

With the busy activity of fishing subsiding, there was once more time to drink in the beauty of nature about me. The warm, penetrating rays of sunshine on my back throttled the grief welling up just inside my heart. One just simply couldn't see "all darkness" in such an exquisite setting. Despite the loneliness I felt, and the fact that it was the 22nd, as I drank in the picturesque scene I was forced to admit that life still held so much pleasure and beauty for me. My little one ran by, his white curls contrasting sharply with a bronze back, his jeans rolled up to his knees, wading along the water's edge in quest of snails, shells, funny bugs, and pretty pebbles. This little life and that of his seven brothers and sisters were such beautiful

160

extensions of the love I had known. They had been a real balm of healing.

Yes, the day was better. I could reach out to memories again, memories which until now had been too painful in their contrast of "what is" and "what had been." The years rolled by; past anniversaries glided before me.

We had always celebrated our anniversaries quite simply. Usually it was just a dinner out. To me that was no little event. Many years, because of limited budget, it was the only one in the whole year. Actually even this one time was a concession on Dad's part. He never could figure out what was so wonderful about a restaurant meal when he had married "the best cook on this side of the Mississippi." (His mother lived on the other side, so he was on safe ground.) But we went anyway because I enjoyed it and he knew I did. Each time we ended the day in a special way, first a prayer of thankfulness to God for our love, our home and our family, followed by a reaffirmation of our love for one another. Just a simple celebration, yet so wonderful. Except for two occasions, we continued this pattern year after year.

Those two anniversaries did not seem so wonderful at the time — yet I will always remember them as best! Our eighth anniversary occurred at a time when I was sure things couldn't get worse. I was nine months pregnant — the sixth pregnancy in eight years — and it was a difficult one. It started with the usual morning sickness which lasted for weeks and weeks. Then a fall caused the last several months to become agony; every movement and step brought searing pain. With five lively youngsters there were just too many steps. To top everything, the third week in June three of our little girls became ill with the measles —

very, very ill. For three days and nights I stood at their bedsides, cooling hot, feverish bodies with sponge baths, running with cold liquids to soothe parched throats, dashing time after time with the basin to the wee one, whose stomach always reacted so violently to high fevers. How I looked forward to the maid (we called her a hired girl) we had engaged to begin the next week.

"Why did we have to have so many babies, and never be able to afford household help for more than a few weeks after the baby arrived?"

The fevers subsided a bit on the 21st, and I made arrangements with a baby-sitter so that we could keep our usual dinner date. I was so exhausted that just getting away for a meal would have been pure bliss.

The morning of the 22nd came, and along with it one of the most severe migraine headaches I had ever suffered. It was no use; everytime I raised my head, I needed the basin. From previous experience I knew that I would be very fortunate to be about the next day. Forgotten in the torture was our anniversary and our dinner.

The family had managed cheese sandwiches and cornflakes at noon. I felt guilty thinking that their supper would probably be cornflakes and cheese sandwiches — switched for variety. Shuffling awkwardly across the kitchen, I managed with the aid of my helpful "well" little daughter to set the table. I found a few leftovers and cold cuts to add to the meager meal.

Then she arrived (the maid who was to start the next week), just as the men were about to come in for supper. With a stiffly-memorized and well-rehearsed speech she announced, "I decided I can't help after all, it's not the pay or anything, it's just too much work!"

"But," I stammered, "if there wasn't work I wouldn't need you. I need help worse than anybody."

No amount of pleading or pressure changed her mind.

"It's too much work," she quoted again, and then quickly left.

At first I was too numb to comprehend the situation completely. Then the realization of how unlikely it was that I would find another maid began to dawn on me. The storm broke. The fatigue, lack of sleep, the difficult pregnancy, and the weakness from the day's nausea all came to a head. I broke into sobbing over which I had no control. A few tears simply could not wash away the utter frustration and discouragement welling within me. All night long I continued in convulsive, hysterical sobs, knowing for certain (I smile at it now) that things couldn't be worse.

Several times Marvin tried to console me. He began by promising to help me all he could. I knew that he would. Few husbands were as capable as he when it came to feeding babies and changing diapers. But he was a busy farmer and I knew how little time there would be left for helping me.

Later he tried another technique: "I hope someday she has five kids and needs help — maybe she'll remember." That line of reasoning also failed to stop the racking sobs.

Finally, much later, he pleaded with me to stop for the baby's sake.

"If you don't stop you're likely to wind up in the maternity ward tonight. You are in no shape for that," he warned. "Honey, please try to sleep."

Wisely he said no more and left me to weep far into

163

the early morning hours, when sheer exhaustion released the tension and sleep took over.

The next day fared better. There was still little likelihood of household help, but the tears had washed away the resentment and things looked brighter. Neither the family nor Marvin mentioned my behavior of the previous night. I'm sure on my page numbered June 22, 1958, in the *Book Of Life,* the Holy Spirit must have shaken his head as he inserted, "Oh, you of little faith." Incidentally, God did provide, in His time, the loveliest young lady I ever had to help me. I simply could never remember to place my needs before Him and then wait for "His time."

The next evening before retiring, I tried to apologize softly by saying, "Oh, Marv, yesterday was our anniversary, and I never remembered. I didn't even tell you that I loved you."

"Honey," he smiled wryly, "if you'd told me yesterday that you loved me, I'd never believe you again." Then after a slight pause he added quietly, "but it's not too late to tell me now, is it?"

Swiftly I flew to his waiting embrace, hot tears of shame spilling over. I bite my lips remembering. . . .

It is good — good to have known a love which didn't need my sunnyside up all the time, a love which kept on loving when I wasn't lovable, a love which gives me a better understanding of the Father's love for His completely undeserving children.

Recollection of that anniversary triggered to mind another incident like that, the time I called him from his busy, overloaded schedule to tell him that he simply must help me with my "crisis." The "crisis" was a huge laundry, a machine filled with hot, soapy water, and nothingness when I pushed the switch to start the agitator. "It's the switch," I explained, "see, when I push the button nothing happens."

Carefully Marvin began removing the entire front panel. There was no other way to get at the wires to the switch. With exacting care he checked each wire and rechecked it. Finding nothing amiss, he replaced all the parts. Still nothing happened when he pushed the button. Once more he repeated the entire procedure. As he began replacing all the parts for a second time, he paused suddenly, and looking up at me, straight in the eye, he asked, "You wouldn't have called me away from my work to fix this before you checked the fuse box, now would you?"

It took just one tiny new fuse to send the machine purring away at its task. Walking disdainfully toward the kitchen door, he glanced back and muttered, "and they tell me I'm supposed to love you." But I caught that little twinkle as he paused there; I knew that he still did.

It was all because of the farm, or the way we farmed it, that we didn't go out to dinner the next anniversary either. We were just small-scale operators and it wasn't financially feasible to purchase all the new, modern harvesting equipment such as hay balers and grain combines. Our acreage was just too small to warrant spending several thousand dollars for machinery which would be used for only a few hours a year. On the other hand it was also impractical to use the old-fashioned equipment, thus taking many days away from Marvin's good-paying, part-time construction job. Our solution was to hire a nearby neighbor to do the job for us. He had large, modern equipment, and it actually was a good arrangement, except that all our harvesting was done on the other man's free time. So it was with a sinking heart that on the 20th of June, Marvin was instructed to begin mowing the hay. One day to cut, one day to dry — simple arithmetic made it plain which day we'd be baling hay — the 22nd. "It isn't fair," I protested, "Last year we never got to celebrate either. I was so counting on this year."

"Well, I suppose you could pray for rain," Marvin drawled. "All our hay would be ruined, but we won't be haying!" He stalked out to the shed where the mower was, shaking his head at that impractical "woman sentimentality."

I'm not quite sure yet if I hoped for rain or sunshine, but I guess it wouldn't have made a great deal of difference. Thursday the 22nd blossomed out to a hot, dry, windy day. I knew even before my husband said so, that I had better forget the plans for our dinner. Actually I was a little relieved. After totaling the check book the day before, there really weren't sufficient funds for a night out. At least I wouldn't have to tell him that on our anniversary.

"It isn't fair," I said to myself. "If I'm not sick, I'm pregnant; when I'm not pregnant there is an empty bank account or the baling of hay. Is just one day (our day) out of the whole year asking too much? Well, if we can't celebrate *out* at least we can celebrate *in*. Sure, why not?"

We had had our dinner at noon, with three extra men at the table — baked ham, scalloped potatoes, cabbage salad, and apple pie; but by the time the day's work was finished we could use another. The idea grew and snowballed. There were plenty of old hens in the freezer and nice fresh strawberries still unpicked in the garden. (Wouldn't they taste good with some delicious home-made ice cream and angel food cake?) I had planned to bake that cake for the men's afternoon tea, but I could give them

166

sandwiches instead. It would mean work, lots of hard, hot work, but we'd celebrate come hayin' or empty bank accounts!

The little girls were delighted with all the fuss. They helped me place our "company" china and the best silver on the fancy linen cloth we kept just for special occasions. Their faces lighted up with expectancy as I decorated the cake with red roses and nine pink candles. Marvin finally came in much later that evening, tired and hot from the long, hard day in the mow, and from milking the seemingly endless number of cattle expecting the same care and routine as on any other day, but he was greeted with six excited faces glowing in the warm candlelight. I had managed a quick shower and a pretty dress too.

"It looks real pretty, Hon." His eyes shone with appreciation for my efforts. "Does this mean that I have to dress too? All the way?"

"All the way! We are the honored guests."

He returned shortly in white shirt and dress trousers. Quickly he took his accustomed seat at the table. The children were delighted with the big party; we were all gay, despite the strenuous day. When I appeared with the cake the children took the cue and began singing, "Happy Anniversary." After the rounds of ice cream, cake, and strawberries, they all agreed that this was the best anniversary yet. "Their best no doubt, but was it mine?" I wondered as I carried away the large stack of dirty dinner plates.

Then, while carrying in Dad's last cup of coffee my glance fell upon his bare feet resting comfortably in those old slippers — the sloppy ones he would not part with because the fur lining was so nice and soft. How irrestible they must have appeared to his tired, aching feet — feet

167

which had been active in love's labor for nearly sixteen hours that day. I smiled remembering his "all the way?"

"Daddy, when you blew out the candles did you make a wish?" Emily wanted to know.

"You don't make wishes at anniversaries do you, Mom?" Dad inquired. "You know what I'd ask for if I did make one? Just this kids, just this: all of you and your mother — just like this always. I suppose that would be asking for time to stand still."

"Time to stand still." I was to hear him repeat these words once again — much later. It was more than a wish then — something between a prayer and a sigh. We were seated at a beautiful wayside park on that late October afternoon. It was Indian summer. All of nature was bursting with the brilliant gold, reds, scarlets, and browns of autumn. It was his autumn too, we both knew that; each knew that the other knew. We did not talk of it. The scenery there at the crest of Cascade Mountain had been so inviting that we had decided to pause there to drink in the exquisite beauty as well as to refresh ourselves with sandwiches and lemonade.

"I hear water, listen!" whispered Linda. Brooks, streams, and glens held such fascination for the children. With sandwiches still in hand they dashed off to explore the area further. Marvin and I remained sitting there in all the golden splendor, watching the children dash through the rustling leaves, into the wooded area seeking the trickling stream. We heard their squeals of delight at their discovery. Grasping my hand tightly, he whispered quietly, "Oh God, if time could just stand still." Ten days later he was gone — time stood still.

After that anniversary celebration I had neither the energy left, nor the time to analyze that warm 'all-is-right' feeling which I hugged to my heart. I was simply a woman fulfilled. The joy — the inexplicable joy — these children, his children, "like olive plants about our table," and a man's undying love. There came the realization that I had succeeded in making his life comfortable, so comfortable that he would ask for time to stand still inspite of sixteen-hour work days and an empty bank account — it was as comfortable as bedroom slippers at an anniversary party.

If for each of us life holds a receptable into which just so much joy and bliss are measured, then I know the Keeper of the Great Fountain above must have spilled as He poured into mine. That cup was already overflowing eight years ago.

I sighed as I remember that rewarding day, a day I might have missed if I hadn't been willing to salvage the threads of broken anticipation and reweave them. Perhaps successful living comes chiefly to those who are most adept at turning shattered dreams and hopes into enchanting new patterns. I thought my family doctor was cruel when he told me shortly after Marvin died, "Listen Gladys, Marvin's dead, that part of your life is gone. You can't live with the past nor with the dead and still remain alive yourself. You must walk ahead now, toward life." Oh, I thought he was cruel. I realize now that he was simply telling me in his words to pick up the pieces and start again.

Today, I can see the value of those pieces. I have my eight beautiful children, four lovely young daughters who are patient and understanding; four little boys keeping life going at a fast, exciting, varied pace, with never a dull moment.

Today I can reach out to memories too, beautiful memories which can only encourage me to go on. And I have friends. Good friends. Friends who have taken time to bring messages of joy and encouragement. Many of these friendships have been made far stronger because they filled a time of need. Always at my side are helpful neighbors and concerned relatives.

God opened many windows when he closed the door of marriage for me. Since Marvin's death I have been able to acquire my B.S. degree, which opens new fields of endeavor. Today I have the thrill of knowing that in a few months I shall begin a part-time teaching appointment. This profession in turn will provide a new social environment and active stimulation.

A closer walk with God is one avenue or window which I surely do not want to miss. Best of all, I have gained a new hope — a hope that can grasp the real meaning of the Easter message. It is a hope that can admit (though still painful) that Marvin will not come back, but gives the assurance that I shall go to him. "Until then I'll carry on."

I pick them up again —
These empty slippers old and worn.
Carefully and gently I refill them with tissue,
    and tuck them into their box.
Even as I reach to place them, once more upon the shelf,
I hear a startled cry of pain —
My baby's hurt needs Mama's kiss,
    his fright her reassurance.
Then far-off voices reach me from a distant hill,

Calling, "Watch us Mom, here we come, here we come.
Our sled is much too fast!"
Down tomorrow's halls and aisles I see marching gradua-
tion caps and lacy wedding gowns.
School boys frown from behind their books —
problems for me, the teacher to solve and to work out.
I can hear the aged crying from their prison beds,
"Do not forget us, do not forget."
and mourning widows calling, "Help, please, help!"
Just one last lingering look at these dear objects of my love,
And then I turn and answer quickly,
"I am coming, I am coming"
for *Life* has called me back.